5 minute TORAH

Short on time? We've got you covered.

Messianic insights into the weekly Torah portion

DARREN N. HUCKEY

5 Minute Torah

Copyright © 2017 Darren N. Huckey. All rights reserved.

Publication rights Emet HaTorah.

Publisher grants permission to reference short quotations (fewer than 400 words) in reviews, magazines, newspapers, web sites, or other publications. Requests for permission to reproduce more than 400 words can be made at:

www.emethatorah.com/contact

Unless noted, all scriptural quotations are from The Holy Bible, English Standard Version, copyright © 2001 by Crossway Bibles, a division of Good News Publishers. Used by permission. All rights reserved.

Cover Design: Darren Huckey

ISBN-13: 978-0-9899991-3-7

Emet HaTorah

PO Box 28281, Macon, GA 31221-8281 | USA

www.emethatorah.com

Comments and questions: www.emethatorah.com/contact

Messianic insights into the weekly Torah portion

Darren N. Huckey

Kaleb, Kai, Boaz, Einya, & Miryam—
May you, your children, and your children's children bring tikkun to this broken world through a life of Torah strengthened by the merits of our Master Yeshua.

Contents

Introduction 1
Parashat B'reisheet 11
Parashat Noach 15
Parashat Lech Lecha 19
Parashat Vayeira 23
Parashat Chayei Sarah 27
Parashat Toldot 31
Parashat Vayeitze 35
Parashat Vayishlach 39
Parashat Vayeishev 43
Parashat Mikeitz 47
Parashat Vayigash 51
Parashat Vayechi 55
Parashat Shemot 59
Parashat Va'era 63
Parashat Bo 67
Parashat Beshalach 71
Parashat Yitro 75
Parashat Mishpatim 79
Parashat Terumah 83
Parashat Tetzaveh 87
Parashat Ki Tisa 91
Parashat Vayakhel 95
Parashat Pekudei 99
Parashat Vayikra 103
Parashat Tzav 107
Parashat Shemini 111
Parashat Tazria 115

Parashat Metzora 119
Parashat Acharei Mot 123
Parashat Kedoshim 127
Parashat Emor 131
Parashat Behar 135
Parashat Bechukotai 137
Parashat Bamidbar 141
Parashat Nasso 145
Parashat Beha'alotcha 149
Parashat Shelach 153
Parashat Korach 157
Parashat Chukat 161
Parashat Balak 165
Parashat Pinchas 169
Parashat Mattot 173
Parashat Massei 177
Parashat Devarim 181
Parashat Va'etchanan 185
Parashat Ekev 189
Parashat Re'eh 193
Parashat Shoftim 197
Parashat Ki Tetze 201
Parashat Ki Tavo 205
Parashat Nitzavim 209
Parashat Vayelech 213
Parashat Ha'azinu 217
Parashat Vezot Ha'Bracha 221

Introduction

Introduction

Welcome to the *5 Minute Torah*! Whether you're short on time or just want a quick thought to help you dig deep into the weekly Torah portions, we've got you covered. Each chapter of this book is a brief commentary on the weekly Torah portion that is designed to give you a thought-provoking insight in just five minutes or less every week. Whether you are looking for quick inspiration, a personal challenge, or a brief nugget you can chew on for the week, the *5 Minute Torah* is for you. We want to help you change your life five minutes at a time. We invite you to enter this journey with us to probe the beauty and depth of the Word of God through the weekly Torah portions. Study along with us and use these weekly thoughts to invoke inspiration and imagination in your faith journey.

A Few Notes About This Work

Although this book can be read from cover to cover in a single sitting, it is specifically designed to be a companion for weekly Torah study, whether on an individual basis or in a group setting. It can be used similar to a devotional, or it can be used around the weekly Sabbath table to promote dialogue about the current Torah portion. And although familiarity with the text from the weekly Torah readings is assumed, it is not necessarily required in order for the reader to benefit from the commentaries. However, to get the most understanding out of the commentaries, a thorough review of the weekly Scripture readings is highly recommended. If you are unsure of the current Torah portion, go to www.torahportions.org and click on the "This Week" tab in the menu. This will get you started studying the text and give you the foundation needed to enrich the weekly commentaries.

Below I have addressed a few particular issues for those new to the weekly Torah cycle and studying from a Messianic Jewish perspective. If you are already familiar with the weekly Torah portions, then feel free to skip ahead and jump right into this week's Torah commentary. However, I have also addressed a few things that are specific to this commentary for those who may be conversant with the Torah and its various interpretations, but may wonder about my particular insights or choices of terms. (If you would like to learn about these, they appear toward the end of this introduction.) Having said that, I will now address questions for those who may be new to Torah study.

Why Study Torah?

Many people may ask, "Why should I keep up with the weekly study of the Torah portions?" The Hebrew Bible is comprised of three parts: The Torah, the Prophets, and the Writings. The Torah tells the story of Israel. It begins with the creation of the world and makes its way through the calling of Abraham and the subsequent history of his offspring. The Torah gives us the background material to understand the rest of Scripture. But the Torah isn't just a story. It is also a legal code that documents the terms of Israel's covenant with the Creator. It contains instructions for communal living—including civil laws and ethical principles that are still the backbone of our Judaeo-Christian value system today—and well-known passages like the Ten Commandments and the Golden Rule: "You shall love your neighbor as yourself" (Leviticus 19:18). It also includes ritual laws about sacrifices, holy days, dietary restrictions, and various other ceremonies.

Since the days of Moses, the Torah has been the rule of life and standard of godliness for God's chosen people, Israel. Unlike other legal documents, its legislation touches on every aspect of human existence. Rather than being concerned merely with civil and ritual interactions, the Torah is also concerned with the condition of the heart. The Shema, the foundational declaration of Jewish faith, declares, "Hear, O Israel: The LORD our God, the LORD is one. You shall love the LORD your God with all your heart and with all your soul and with all your might" (Deuteronomy 6:5). The God of Abraham, Isaac, Jacob, and Yeshua desires to connect with the heart of man. The study and application of the principles of Torah work toward this goal of transforming us as a person and connecting our hearts with the heart of God.

Studying the Torah on a continual basis also creates a solid foundation upon which our understanding of the rest of the Scriptures can rest. It creates a means by which we can discern fraudulent or careless interpretations of Scripture. By knowing the original revelation upon which all subsequent Scripture rests, we can more confidently navigate the Prophets, the Writings, and the Apostolic Scriptures to arrive at understandings that are in agreement with Scripture as a whole, rather than developing theological constructs independent from the greater Scriptural context. In short, studying Torah helps us to develop a proper orientation to the rest of the Scriptures.

What Is A Torah Portion?

The weekly study of the Torah—the five books of Moses, Genesis through Deuteronomy—has been a part of Jewish religious life since antiquity. According to tradition, the prophet Ezra began the systematic study of the Torah after the return of the Israelite exiles from Babylon. This practice persists even today. Every year, hundreds of thousands, if not millions, of people across the world undertake a reading of the entire Torah. You can visit any synagogue in the

Introduction

world on any Sabbath and hear the weekly Torah portion being read, studied, and expounded upon.

The weekly readings are integrally tied to the Hebrew calendar, ensuring that the cycle will begin anew at the same time each fall during the festival of Sukkot (Tabernacles). We celebrate this renewal through a mini-festival called Simchat Torah (the Rejoicing of the Torah).

The Torah has been broken down into 54 portions called parashot (parashah, singular). The parashot are divided so that each parashah covers a particular theme, but is small enough to be digestible. You can find these readings online. We recommend a couple of sources. The first is one I mentioned earlier: www.torahportions.org. This site was created by our friends at First Fruits of Zion and includes weekly readings of the Gospels arranged in chronological order, along with their own weekly commentaries. The second is www.Hebcal.com. Here you can view the weekly readings and actually download a calendar to your computer or mobile device. It does not have any New Testament readings.

Why Are There Sometimes Double Portions?

Sometimes two portions are read together for a particular week. This is because the Jewish calendar is a lunar calendar that uses a solar correction to calculate the months of the year. Because it is primarily based on the cycles of the moon, the Jewish calendar is generally about eleven days shorter than the solar year. Every two to three years is a leap year, and an additional month is added to the calendar to keep it in sync with the solar year. The readings are therefore broken down to accommodate for the additional weeks added to the year. Therefore, during a non-leap year, some of the weekly readings are combined. Other factors also come into play, but this is the basic reason behind the double Torah portions.

What About Haftarah and Apostolic Readings?

In addition to the weekly Torah portion, a passage from one of the books of the prophets is read. This reading is called the haftarah. These passages have been chosen because of some type of thematic connection to the weekly parashah, even though the connection may sometimes not be understood by a casual reading.

In the last few decades, some have attempted to introduce an accepted system of readings pulling from the Apostolic Scriptures (i.e., the New Testament). Two systems in particular have gained popularity. The first system, devised by Dr. David Stern (author of The Complete Jewish Bible), draws on a theme from the weekly parashah and attempts to connect a passage from the Apostolic Scriptures to it. These readings are generally brief and are designed for inclusion in a liturgical setting.

The second system, created by First Fruits of Zion, serves a similar purpose. This system primarily uses passages from the Gospels, which are thematically linked to the parashah, except during the three weeks between Tzom Tammuz and Tisha B'Av and the seven weeks of comfort following Tisha B'Av. On these weeks, the Gospel sections tie into the haftarah portion.

Notes On The Commentary

I do not claim originality in my interpretations. Many of the *5 Minute Torah* commentaries are drawn from insights of classic commentators such as Rashi, Rambam, Ramban, etc., Many insights have been gleaned from chassidic interpretation as well. However, since my perspective is through the lens of the teachings of Yeshua of Nazareth and his Apostles, my insights may take a different dimension

Introduction

than the original interpretation. I will often use traditional interpretations as a springboard for additional insights that have relevant meaning to followers of Yeshua.

Even though I am a Messianic Gentile and not Jewish, I have intentionally chosen to use certain phrases that reflect an orientation that places Messianic Judaism within greater Judaism. For example, I chose to use the phrase "our sages" when referring to the sages of Israel, in order to show the continuity between Judaism and Messianic Judaism. When a non-Jew comes to Yeshua and adopts Messianic Judaism as his religious practice, his religion is a sect within Judaism rather than an opposing religion apart from it. This is the reason behind the term Messianic Judaism. It is a branch of Judaism, albeit with Yeshua as the Messiah of Israel at the center. By continuing to use exclusionary phrases that position Messianic Judaism, and Messianic Gentiles in particular, outside the scope of Judaism, we will never find identity and take ownership within the scope of greater Judaism. It will continue to be a dichotomy of "us" and "them," rather than one religion with multiple expressions. Do Gentiles have different obligations than the native-born? Yes. However, we must keep in mind that Gentiles who have adopted Messianic Judaism practice a form of Judaism that is appropriate for non-Jews and congruent with historical Judaism.

Also, at the end of the commentaries for the last portions of each book—for instance, Parashat Vayechi is the last portion for the book of Genesis—I have included the traditional words, "*Chazak! Chazak! V'nitchazeik!* Be strong! Be strong! And may we be strengthened!" This tradition is a reminder that although we have completed a book of the Torah, there is still more to learn. In the modern era we might say something like, "You're doing great! There are even better things ahead!" I have chosen to include this phrase at the end of these particular portions as both a reminder that these portions conclude a book of the Torah, and as an encouragement to continue learning with zeal.

Lastly, the Jewish-published Bible and the Christian-published Bible at times differ in how chapters and verses are numbered. Wherever there is a discrepancy between the chapter and verse in a referenced passage, I have made the Jewish numbering the default but added the Christian numbering in brackets (e.g. Genesis 28:10-32:3[2]).

May the words of Ben Bag-Bag and Ben Heh-Heh remind us that we must continually labor over the Torah to search out its treasures, and that the rewards we gain from it will be commensurate with our effort:

> Ben Bag-Bag used to say of the Torah: Turn it and turn it again, for everything is in it. Pore over it, and wax gray and old over it. Stir not from it for you can have no better rule than it. Ben Heh-Heh used to say: According to the effort is the reward. (Avot 6:26)

May the Holy One of Israel bless you as you engage His Holy Word and find application to live a life of righteousness before Him and before others. May the prayer of our hearts continually be in agreement with King David's words: "Open my eyes, that I may behold wondrous things out of your Torah" (Psalm 119:18). And may our lives bear the fruit of righteousness so that we may fulfill the desire of our Master, that those around us may see our good works and give glory to our Father in Heaven (Matthew 5:16).

Darren Huckey
27 Elul 5777
September 18, 2017

Commentary

Parashat B'reisheet

GENESIS 1:1-6:8

First Light

Parashat B'reisheet is an intriguing Torah portion. This parashah contains so many facets of the Creation account to explore that it would take a lifetime to unravel it. For instance, on the first day of Creation, we read about the creation of light:

> And God said, "Let there be light," and there was light. And God saw that the light was good. And God separated the light from the darkness. God called the light Day, and the darkness he called Night. And there was evening and there was morning, the first day. (Genesis 1:3–5)

Although light was created on the first day, the sun, moon, and stars were not created until the fourth day. If these luminaries were not created until the fourth day, then what was the light that illuminated the first three days? Fortunately, we have the insights of our sages from the last two millennia to help us peer into the deep mysteries of these events. Rashi, the famous medieval commentator, says this passage cannot be properly understood without outside commentary, particularly the midrash.

What does the midrash have to say about this passage? More

than we have time to cover here. But the main concept we need to understand is that the light that was first spoken into existence is unique and distinct from the light produced by the luminaries. It was a special, pure light that radiated from God himself. The Torah gives us a clue about the quality of this light when it says, "And God saw that the light was good." It was the first of all Creation to have this special designation of "good." According to Rabbi Elazar, in a midrash called Yalkut Shimoni, the light that God created on the first day was used by Adam to look from one end of the universe to the other. It was something extremely special.

Because of its uniqueness, its sanctity was more than a soon-to-be fallen world could handle. Therefore, the Torah tells us that "God separated the light from the darkness." The midrash explains that this separation was not merely an untangling of light from darkness, but its complete removal. Where did this light go? The midrash tells us this:

> It is stored up for the righteous in the Messianic future, as it says (Isaiah 30:26), "Moreover the light of the moon shall be as the light of the sun, and the light of the sun shall be sevenfold, as the light of the seven days." (Genesis Rabbah 3:6)

For now, that light continues to be hidden away "until the time of reformation" (Hebrews 9:10). When this light is returned to the earth, the New Jerusalem will shine it forth to all of creation, as it is said, "The city has no need of sun or moon to shine on it, for the glory of God gives it light, and its lamp is the Lamb" (Revelation 21:23). Darkness will be vanquished and the supernal light of Creation will return to illuminate the world forever, as it says, "And night will be no more. They will need no light of lamp or sun, for the Lord God will be their light, and they will reign forever and ever" (Revelation 22:5).

As we longingly await the arrival of that Holy Eternal Light, let us continue to shine forth the light of the Torah and of our Messiah so that the world will see our good deeds—a glimpse of this supernatural light—and glorify our Father in Heaven. One day the True Light will be revealed in all of its glory. Until then, may our actions be a reflection of its splendor.

Parashat Noach

GENESIS 6:9-11:32

Leaving A Legacy

Parashat Noach opens with the words, "These are the generations of Noah. Noah was a righteous man, blameless in his generation. Noah walked with God" (Genesis 6:9). In this passage, "generations" is the Hebrew word *toldot* (תולדת). The word toldot is most often used in the Scriptures in relationship to genealogy, since its primary meaning is "descendants" or "offspring." For instance, toward the end of this week's parashah we read, "These are the generations of Shem" (Genesis 11:10). Immediately following is a list of Shem's descendants. The pattern repeats with Terah, the father of Abraham, saying, "Now these are the generations of Terah" (Genesis 11:27), followed by a list of his children. The same goes for the lists of the sons of Ishmael in Genesis 25, etc.

However, in the case of the Bible's description of Noah (and a few other select individuals), rather than listing his children, his character traits are listed. The Scriptures appear to be emphasizing that, more than his literal offspring—the very ones that would repopulate the world after the flood—Noah's legacy was to be found in his character. The Scriptures list three "offspring" of Noah: his righteousness, his blamelessness, and his relationship with God. Let's briefly explore these concepts.

Parashat Noach

Noah was righteous. What does this mean? Righteousness is a legal status by which one person is declared to be in right relationship with another. This means that Noah held to the standard that the LORD had given him, as it is written, "The LORD tests the righteous, but his soul hates the wicked and the one who loves violence. ... For the LORD is righteous; he loves righteous deeds; the upright shall behold his face." (Psalm 11:5, 7). When the LORD told Noah to enter into the ark, He reminded Noah of his righteousness by saying, "Go into the ark, you and all your household, for I have seen that you are righteous before me in this generation" (Genesis 7:1).

Noah was blameless. What does this mean? A person is blameless when they avoid the things that displease God. For instance, when the Children of Israel were about to enter into the Promised Land, the LORD commanded them saying, "You shall be blameless before the LORD your God" (Deuteronomy 18:13). He desired that they not follow the abominations of the nations they were about to dispossess. The LORD qualifies what it means to be blameless by saying, "For these nations, which you are about to dispossess, listen to fortune-tellers and to diviners. But as for you, the LORD your God has not allowed you to do this" (Deuteronomy 18:14). Although there was wickedness all around him, Noah stood firm and did not succumb to the temptation to reduce his religious observance to the lowest common denominator of his environment.

Noah walked with God. What does this mean? God desires that His children walk with him. The prophet Micah tells us, "He has told you, O man, what is good; and what does the LORD require of you but to do justice, and to love kindness, and to walk humbly with your God?" (Micah 6:8). Walking with God is an idiom for faithfulness, as the Scriptures tell us, "Ephraim has surrounded me with lies, and the house of Israel with deceit, but Judah still walks with

God and is faithful to the Holy One" (Hosea 11:12).

Although Noah lived in a wicked generation, he was a righteous man, blameless in his generation, and he walked with God. What can we say of ourselves? Are we righteous, blameless, and walking with God? How will our toldot be remembered?

Parashat Lech Lecha

GENESIS 12:1-17:27

Partnering With God

In Parashat Lech Lecha we begin learning about a character by the name of Abram. As we know, his name will eventually be changed to Abraham, and our knowledge of his life is pivotal to our understanding of God's plan for humanity. In fact, the entire Scriptures hinge around this one person. When we read this week's portion, Abraham's courageous faith immediately becomes apparent when he leaves everything behind and moves to the land of Canaan in order to obey God's command. This is the first of several of Abraham's trials we read about in this small section of Genesis.

The next trial we learn about is his encounter with Pharaoh and how he attempts to protect his family from the Egyptians. Then we read of the dispute between his nephew Lot's shepherds and his own, and the trial of dividing the land between his nephew and himself. We also read about his trial of rescuing Lot when he and his household were captured by invading armies. The next trial is overcoming the pain of being childless and results in the taking of his wife's servant Hagar as an additional wife through which his son Ishmael is born. The last trial in this portion is the commandment for Abraham to circumcise himself and all the males of his household. But there is something unique about how this particular trial is introduced.

When the LORD instructed Abraham in regard to circumcision, He first said, "I am God Almighty; walk before me, and be perfect, that I may make my covenant between me and you, and may multiply you greatly" (Genesis 17:1–2). When God made His covenant of circumcision with Abraham, the intention was to make Abraham something greater than what he was. Somehow this act of obedience through altering his physical nature would produce in Abraham a partnership with God that could not be achieved otherwise. This concept is difficult to grasp, but it's one that deserves our attention.

Circumcision is a volatile topic these days. The secular world sees it as a barbaric and cruel practice. Many Christians view it negatively as well, due to Paul's statement that in regard to salvation it is a "mutilat[ion] of the flesh" (Philippians 3:2). But we have to remember that the God of the universe is the one who instructed Abraham and all future generations of his descendants to undergo this transformation. But why would God want man to do such a thing if He created us *uncircumcised* to begin with? The answer connects us back to the introduction of His covenant of circumcision: "I am God Almighty; walk before me, and be perfect." Our sages said that, before his circumcision, Abraham was not whole (i.e. "perfect"). Once he was circumcised, however, he became whole (Midrash Tanchuma on Genesis 17:1).

God desires to partner with man in order to bless him and to do great things in this world. When man partners with God to accomplish wonderful things—even in seemingly minute things—we are fulfilling our calling to walk before Him, striving toward perfection just as Abraham did. For instance, God did not create trees that produce bread (though that would be nice, wouldn't it?). Instead, God provides only the grain for the bread. Man must do the rest. We must harvest the grain, thresh and winnow it, grind it, mix it with other ingredients, and then bake it before we have a delicious loaf of bread. By doing so, man partners with God to create something beautiful and beneficial for humanity.

The same is true in our spiritual lives. Although we may be born a certain way, we must realize that we are not supposed to remain that way. We should never be satisfied with "the way we are," but should always strive to become something more than how we were created. Just as we work together with God to create bread, and just as Abraham worked with God to circumcise all the males of his house, so should we work with God to alter ourselves in ways that make us more like our Creator. It's not an easy task, but through much patience and diligence, we can partner with the LORD to become the person He envisioned when He created us.

Parashat Vayeira

GENESIS 18:1-22:24

Our Father Abraham

Many people are familiar with the children's song, "Father Abraham." It begins, "Father Abraham had many sons, and many sons had Father Abraham. I am one of them, and so are you. So, let's just praise the Lord." Through repetition and a series of choreographed movements, this song ingrains the concept into a child that Vayeira, this week's Torah portion, is indeed true. Abraham did become the father of many nations and is affectionately called *Avraham Avinu*, Our Father Abraham. Paul says that Abraham is "the father of all who believe" (Romans 4:12). We who have put our trust in Yeshua have become the spiritual offspring of Abraham, the father of our faith.

According to our Torah portion, the LORD chose Abraham as the father of many nations for specific reasons:

> The LORD said, "Shall I hide from Abraham what I am about to do, seeing that Abraham shall surely become a great and mighty nation, and all the nations of the earth shall be blessed in him? For I have chosen him, that he may command his children and his household after him to keep the way of the LORD by doing righteousness and justice, so that

the LORD may bring to Abraham what he has promised him." (Genesis 18:17–19)

Abraham was chosen in order "that he may command his children and his household after him to keep the way of the LORD by doing righteousness (*tzedakah*) and justice (*mishpat*)." In Hebrew, doing righteousness is a synonym for taking care of those in need. And when native Hebrew speakers use the word *tzedakah*, righteousness, most often they mean charity. By Yeshua's day this concept was in full force. In Matthew 6, Yeshua uses the word in this manner when he says, "Beware of practicing your righteousness before other people" (Matthew 6:1). Justice, *mishpat*, on the other hand, often connotes strictness. The midrash tells a story to explain one way that Abraham did righteousness and justice.

Abraham and Sarah were known for their hospitality. According to the midrash, they used to take in travelers and give them food and lodging. Once they had enjoyed a wonderful meal, Abraham would ask them to give thanks to Hashem. If they refused, then he would demand payment for the food they had consumed. Because he demanded such a high rate for the food, they would be happy to bless his God. Abraham began with tzedakah (charity), but would add to it mishpat (strictness).

According to a more literal reading of the text, however, the righteousness and justice Abraham would teach to his children would be in relationship to the basic principles of Torah ethics. Even though the Torah had not yet been given to Israel, Abraham would live out its very basic principles and teach his children to do likewise. His example would set the pattern for his descendants after him, as it is said, "The deeds of the fathers are the portents for the children." Therefore, to be a child of Abraham is to follow in his footsteps.

How can we follow in our father Abraham's footsteps? Hospitality is an obvious way. Obedience is another. We could list a host of others. May we look to Avraham Avinu as an example of our faith, following his lead at living a life that is pleasing to Hashem and passing that life down to the next generation.

Parashat Chayei Sarah

GENESIS 23:1–25:18

The Eternal Life of Sarah

This week's Torah portion begins by giving us the lifespan of Sarah:

> And these were the life of Sarah: one hundred years, twenty years and seven years; the years of the life of Sarah. (Genesis 23:1)

Since this portion is titled *Chayei Sarah*, "The Life of Sarah," we would expect to read more about the life of Sarah. But the very next words we read are, "And Sarah died." It's not quite what we expect of our Torah portion.

Despite the fact that we begin our portion reading about the death of Sarah, we can still learn something about her life. Although our translations render the first verse so that it reads better in English, in Hebrew this verse contains an unusual repetition. The same phrase, *chayei Sarah*, is used two different times: first at the beginning of the verse, and again at the end. This seems redundant. Our sages teach us, however, that the Torah does not waste even a single letter, much less entire words. Therefore, the seemingly redundant expression, "the life of Sarah," must offer us some insight into a deeper meaning of the text. But what is the Torah wanting to teach us through this?

Throughout the Tanach (the Hebrew Scriptures), the concept of life-after-death is not plainly mentioned. This principle is not explicitly mentioned until the Apostolic Scriptures. However, our sages and Apostles had a firm belief in this concept based on their understanding of the Tanach alone. How did they come up with such a strong conviction? Through a careful reading of passages such as these. This passage mentions the life of Sarah twice. Therefore, our sages deduced that the Torah speaks of Sarah's life in this world and her life in the world to come. Although her life in this world had ended, she will one day be resurrected to experience life again. This is also attested to by the Hebrew Scriptures in that the word *chai*, life, is never used in the singular, but always in the plural.

During the first century, the Pharisees and the Sadducees debated the reality of resurrection. The Sadducees, maintaining a literal reading of the Tanach, rejected the notion of resurrection. The Pharisees, however, approached the Scriptures entirely differently and saw the resurrection in numerous passages. Knowing that Yeshua aligned himself doctrinally with the Pharisees, the Sadducees challenged him to provide proof for the resurrection. This was Yeshua's response:

> "And as for the resurrection of the dead, have you not read what was said to you by God: 'I am the God of Abraham, and the God of Isaac, and the God of Jacob'? He is not God of the dead, but of the living." (Matthew 22:31–32)

But his words were not the only evidence he gave. Yeshua eventually settled this debate conclusively with his own resurrection:

But in fact Christ has been raised from the dead, the firstfruits of those who have fallen asleep. For as by a man came death, by a man has come also the resurrection of the dead. (1 Corinthians 15:20–21)

Human beings were created with the capacity to move from one life to the next. Our life does not end once our physical bodies have ceased functioning. Sarah lived a full and meaningful life in this world. At the resurrection she will have life again. But she didn't wait until the resurrection to start living fully. She lived out her years in service to her Creator. Have you begun living yet? If not, what are you waiting for? Life begins now.

Parashat Toldot

GENESIS 25:19-28:9

The Offspring Of Yeshua

This week's parashah begins with the words, "These are the generations of Isaac, Abraham's son: Abraham fathered Isaac" (Genesis 25:19). Like Parashat Noach, this passage uses the word "generations," toldot (תולדת), to begin the story of Isaac's adulthood. As we had described in the story of Noah, toldot is used in the Torah most often in relationship to genealogy, since its primary meaning is "descendants" or "offspring." However, like we discovered of Noah, sometimes a person's character or unique traits is listed as their toldot. This is the case again with Isaac. Rather than beginning with the birth of Jacob and Esau, the Torah describes the toldot of Isaac as, "Abraham fathered Isaac." Why is this?

If we look back just a few chapters to Parashat Vayeira, we are reminded of an event that happened with Sarah in Genesis 20. When Abraham and Sarah were journeying through his land, Abimelech, king of Gerar, abducted Sarah and took her for himself. He intended to make her either a wife or a concubine. However, the Torah explains that "Abimelech had not approached her" (Genesis 20:4) when God appeared to him in a dream and revealed to him that Sarah was married to Abraham. He explained to Abimelech, "It was I who kept you from sinning against me. Therefore I did not let you touch her"

(v. 6). Mortified at the thought of taking another man's wife and paying for it with his life, Abimelech promptly returned Sarah to her husband. After she was returned, Abraham prayed for Abimelech and his household to bear children, because "the LORD had closed all the wombs of the house of Abimelech" (v. 18).

But the story didn't end there. Immediately following, we read about the conception and birth of Isaac. The LORD fulfilled His word to Abraham and blessed him by giving him a son through his wife, Sarah. From a scoffer's perspective, however, it seemed that there may have been some funny business going on. Abraham and Sarah had been married for many, many years and were unable to produce any natural offspring of their own. Now, all of a sudden—after Sarah's abduction by Abimelech and return to Abraham—Sarah is pregnant? Is this really Abraham's child, or does it belong to Abimelech?

Rashi says our opening verse was written in the Torah to resolve this suspicion: "These are the generations of Isaac, Abraham's son: Abraham fathered Isaac." Based on the midrash, he interprets this passage to mean that God made Isaac to look so much like Abraham that his paternity was unquestionable. But not only did Isaac look like Abraham, he acted like him as well. He imitated his father in hospitality, kindness, and faith. The toldot of Isaac was that he was Abraham's son. Because he was the spitting image of his father in both appearance and deeds, there was absolutely no doubt as to who might be his father. Isaac was definitely a product of Abraham.

Often people claim to be toldot of Yeshua. But being his offspring is more than a label. When people examine us, they should see an obvious reflection of our spiritual paternity. Can they see Yeshua in us? Are we a reflection of him? Or do they suspect our spiritual paternity to be of dubious origins? Just as Isaac resembled his father Abraham, disciples of Yeshua should resemble him in more ways than not. When people see us, there should be no question in their minds as to whom we belong. They should automatically say, "They are a disciple of Yeshua."

Parashat Vayeitze

GENESIS 28:10-32:3[2]

The Impact Of The Righteous

Our parashah begins, "Jacob left Beersheba and went toward Haran" (Genesis 28:10). Rashi makes a keen observation on this verse. He asks a question that should be obvious to us: "Why does the Torah mention Jacob's departure from Beersheba?" If we've been paying attention, we should remember that the Torah had just mentioned this fact a few verses prior. Verse seven says, "Jacob had obeyed his father and his mother and gone to Paddan-aram." Haran is located within the region of Paddan-aram. Therefore, we've been told twice within a few sentences that Jacob went toward Haran. If the Torah doesn't waste words, then why does it repeat itself in this case? Rashi says that we are supposed to learn an important lesson through this repetition:

> This tells us that the departure of a righteous man from a place makes an impression, for while the righteous man is in the city, he is its beauty, he is its splendor, he is its majesty. When he departs from there, its beauty has departed, its splendor has departed, its majesty has departed. (Rashi's reference to and quotation of Genesis Rabbah 68:6)

Parashat Vayeitze

According to Rashi, the repetition of Jacob's departure is to teach us "that the departure of a righteous man from a place makes an impression." When Jacob left Beersheba, his absence was felt. The people in that region missed him terribly and realized that his presence made a difference in their lives. When he was with them, nothing was lacking. Maybe they didn't necessarily recognize the benefit of his presence while he was with them and noticed the void only when he departed. Nevertheless, once he had left, his absence was palpable. The departure of a righteous person should be obvious.

This is why Yeshua's departure from this world made such an impression on the entire planet. The complete tzaddik—the completely righteous one—departed from this earth and left an enormous vacuum that no one else will ever be able to fill. The hearts of his disciples felt like they were torn from within them. They wandered about like abandoned children, bemoaning the loss of their beloved rabbi. Yet when he appeared to them after his resurrection, their hearts were ignited once again. They said, "Did not our hearts burn within us while he talked to us on the road, while he opened to us the Scriptures?" (Luke 24:32). In order to fill this vacuum left by his presence, he sent the Comforter, the Holy Spirit, to take his place in the hearts of his followers. Yes, his disciples still long for his return even to this day, but we at least sense his presence through this agent.

Too many times we live our lives with little to no impact on the people around us. Sadly, many times people quit their job, move out of state, or even pass away from this life without many people noticing. For disciples of Yeshua, however, this should not be the case. We should be making a significant impact not only on those closest to us, but also to the world in general. As our Master has told us, a light "hidden under a bushel" doesn't have much influence on the darkness around it. We don't have the luxury of hiding our light. Our job is to reflect the light of our Master and shine it brightly into the world. Do people know that you are a disciple of Yeshua? Have they seen your good works and begun to glorify your Father in heaven? When you're not around, is your absence felt? Or does anyone even notice? Both the presence and the departure of a righteous person should be noticeable.

Parashat Vayishlach

GENESIS 32:4[3]-36:43

The Irrational Lure Of Self-Destruction

This week's parashah covers a lot of territory. We begin reading about Jacob preparing to meet his brother Esau after his departure from the house of Laban. From there we read about his wrestling through the night with what appears to be an angel of God. Jacob then encounters Esau and things go much better than expected. Esau is cordial and Jacob doesn't get killed, so he skirts around his brother's territory and heads over to Succoth. But after this we read of a sad incident in which his daughter, Dinah, is seduced and defiled by a man named Shechem. We will examine this incident a little more closely.

When Shechem first saw Dinah, he immediately desired her. He knew he needed to do whatever it took to get her. Our English translations make it appear that he simply found her alone and had his way with her. It says, "he seized her and lay with her and humiliated [or violated] her" (Genesis 34:2). The next verse, however, seems to indicate that Shechem had a genuine love for Dinah. It says, "And his soul was drawn to Dinah the daughter of Jacob. He loved the young woman and spoke tenderly to her" (Genesis 34:3). Even more confusing is the midrash's account of how Dinah was rescued from Shechem. Commenting on the Torah's account that they "took Dinah out of Shechem's house," Rabbi Judah says, "They dragged her out [against her will] and departed" (Midrash Rabbah 80:11 commenting on Genesis 34:26).

At first, this doesn't seem reasonable. It seems clear from a plain reading of the text that Dinah was being held against her wishes. A quick examination of the Hebrew, however, helps shed light on this. In Hebrew, the phrase, "[he] spoke tenderly to her," in verse three is more literally translated, "he spoke to the heart of the young woman" (*vayidaber al lev hana'ara*). It seems that Shechem was what we call a "smooth talker." Whether their relationship began with this smooth talk or not, it seems clear that Dinah's emotions were being played upon at some point along the way and kept her from leaving him. In today's terminology, we would call situations like this codependency. In a codependent situation, a woman will continually return to her husband after being abused because she believes his love for her is sincere, despite his abusive behavior. This isn't rational behavior.

But Dinah and other women in similar situations are not the only ones who fall prey to the devices of seduction. We all do. If we have ever sinned, then we realize this power, because in order to sin we first have to be deceived into believing we will derive benefit from our sinful actions. Although we may know the harmful effects of our bad choices, making rational decisions is extremely difficult when we are being seduced. We are no longer thinking and acting rationally. We say and do things that we would not do otherwise.

Often our desire for immediate gratification is what gets us to this point. This is often the case when it comes to establishing beneficial habits such as prayer, study, or even exercise. We have a desire to pray, study, or exercise, but rather than stick with our commitment, we fall prey to the allure of distractions that promise to deliver more immediate satisfaction than our original plan.

When and how does it end? It ends when we can keep our eye on the prize that awaits us. If we are constantly distracted from the goal of the Kingdom and the things we must do to pursue it, the enemy will easily seduce us into accomplishing his goal instead. We must be ever vigilant against the deceptions of the enemy and the tricks he implores to lead us down paths we would never travel in our right minds.

Parashat Vayeishev

GENESIS 37:1-40:23

What's In Your Pit?

Parashat Vayeishev begins the story of Joseph. When we first encounter him, he is a seventeen year old young man. We learn that his father, Jacob, had a special love for him above all of his eleven brothers. He was loved so much that his father had given him a special and highly recognizable garment that distinguished him from among his brothers. This disproportionate love stirred up jealousy from his brothers and fostered their resentment toward him. That resentment eventually turned to a genuine hatred of Joseph and caused his brothers to plot to do away with him.

As the story goes, one day Jacob tells Joseph to go out to the land of Shechem where his older brothers were watching over the flock. He was to check in on them and see how they were doing and then report back to his father. His father knew he would give him the scoop on what his other sons were really doing while they were away from home with the flock. His brothers probably called him the Little Snitch. And being his father's spy didn't earn Joseph any brownie points with his brothers. It only stirred up more hatred toward him.

When Joseph finally tracked down his brothers, his presence was not well received. As a matter of fact, when they saw him coming in the distance, they conspired on how they could kill him. Fortunately Reuben, the eldest brother, dissuaded his brothers from actually killing Joseph and instead convinced them to throw him into a pit until he could come up with a plan for what to do with him. The description of their throwing Joseph into the pit, however, is interesting. The Torah says, "And they took him and threw him into a pit. The pit was empty; there was no water in it" (Genesis 37:24). Since the Torah tells us that the pit was empty, why does it have to follow this up by letting us know there was no water in it? Why wasn't it sufficient to simply let us know that the pit was empty?

The word the Torah uses for "pit" here is the Hebrew word *bor*. It can refer to a pit, well, or cistern. Therefore, it would be natural to assume that there would have been water in the bor. However, since there was no water in it, we must ask, "What was in it?" The majority of Jewish commentators on this passage agree that the Torah specifically declares there was no water in the bor in order to let us know that, in place of water, it was filled with snakes and scorpions. If this is the case, being in the pit was no pleasant experience for Joseph.

But if this is true, why didn't the Torah just tell us that there were snakes and scorpions in the pit, rather than leaving it up to deduction for us to figure this out? The answer is that sometimes it is only when we realize what is missing that we discover something else has taken its place. This is especially true when it comes to spiritual matters. Torah is compared to water, as it is said, "Come, everyone who thirsts, come to the waters [of Torah]" (Isaiah 55:1). Each person has a bor within them. It is our head. No one is truly "empty-headed." Our minds are always packed to the max. However, it may not be filled with the proper materials. We should be pouring into ourselves the water of Torah and spiritual matters every day. When we don't, we will easily find that our minds are consumed with the matters, influences, and values of the world. We will wake up one day and realize our minds have been drained of the water of Torah and are a home only to the snakes and scorpions of the world. What's in your pit?

Parashat Mikeitz

GENESIS 41:1–44:17

A Candle In The Darkness

Nearly every year Parashat Mikeitz is read in conjunction with the celebration of Hanukkah. Can we find any parallel or insight in this week's Torah portion that relates to Hanukkah? A few rabbis (particularly Rabbi Yaakov Weinberg) have brought insight into this correlation. Our parashah tells us:

> And Pharaoh said to Joseph, "I have had a dream, and there is no one who can interpret it. I have heard it said of you that when you hear a dream you can interpret it." Joseph answered Pharaoh, "It is not in me; God will give Pharaoh a favorable answer." (Genesis 41:15–16)

In this instance we read that Joseph is brought before Pharaoh to interpret his dream. Pharaoh begins his conversation with Joseph by giving him credit for being able to interpret dreams. Rather than taking credit himself, Joseph deflects this statement and gives proper recognition to God as the true interpreter of dreams. Joseph is a true example of humility. In him we see a firm reliance upon God. He realizes that everything that happens to him—every success and every failure—is in the hands of Heaven. He is only the vessel through

Parashat Mikeitz

which the Creator can do His will. He shined his light before Pharaoh. A single candle amidst the darkness of Egypt.

We see this in the leadership of Judah Maccabee as well:

> And Judah and his brethren saw that evils were multiplied, and that the armies approached to their borders, and they knew the orders the king had given to destroy the people and utterly abolish them. And they said every man to his neighbor, "Let us raise up the low condition of our people, and let us fight for our people, and our sanctuary." And the assembly was gathered that they might be ready for battle, and that they might pray, and ask mercy and compassion. (1 Maccabees 3:42–44)

As he led his small band of freedom fighters in guerrilla warfare tactics against the Greek armies, he knew that their success was entirely in the hands of Heaven. The Greeks outnumbered them and outpowered them, but they knew that victory was not entirely dependent upon themselves. Yes, they would have to do their part, but God was the ultimate determination in the outcome. They chose, therefore, to put their trust in Him:

> It is an easy matter for many to be shut up in the hands of a few, and there is no difference in the sight of the God of heaven to deliver with a great multitude, or with a small company. For the success of war is not in the multitude of the army, but strength comes from heaven. They come against us with an insolent multitude, and with pride, to destroy us and our wives and our children, and to take our spoils. But we will fight for our lives and our laws, and the

Lord himself will overthrow them before our face, but as for you, fear them not. (1 Maccabees 3:18–22)

The result was that their small and tattered armies were able to bring victory to their people against a great foe. The Maccabees could have commemorated their victory over the mighty Greek armies through a traditional victory march year after year. They could have had a monument built in their name. They could have done a number of things that would have been self-focused and for their own glory. But they chose to do something that would bring honor to the One who had given them the victory. They chose to have an eight-day celebration of the miracles that God performed for them. They chose to bring light into the world through a yearly reminder of the rededication of God's Holy House. We call that reminder Hanukkah.

When we light the Hanukkah lights this week, let us remember all of the miracles that our God has done for us. Joseph continually remembered and gave glory to the One whom it was due. So did the Maccabees. Let us do the same and thereby shine some light into this dark world around us.

Parashat Vayigash

GENESIS 44:18-47:27

Bitter or Better

Ani Yosef—"I am Joseph." You could have heard a pin drop when Joseph spoke those two Hebrew words to his brothers. Their mouths fell open and their jaws nearly hit the floor. Their eyes bulged as they strained to recognize their younger brother hidden beneath the Egyptian garb. Confusion and despair rushed over them from head to foot in an instant. An icy chill coursed through their veins at the sudden realization that the man who stood in front of them—the second most powerful man in Egypt—was the one they had betrayed over twenty years previously. The next few seconds played out as if they were in slow motion as they began processing those two words. Their minds rewound the moment and zoomed in on his lips as he spoke, "Ani Yosef!" "Did he really just say what we think we heard?" It probably seemed like an eternity as a million thoughts, fears, and regrets all collided in their minds simultaneously. Time stood frozen solid as the implications of this simple statement firmly landed on each of them.

We are so dead ... they probably thought to themselves. *The ghost of Joseph has come back to haunt us and take us down to the grave with him! This explains why he has been so cruel to us! We are doomed!* It probably took them a few moments more to realize that Joseph had said something else also. Something about their father. What was it? Oh, yes ... he said, "Is my father still alive?" But they couldn't answer. They were literally speechless. They were still in shock at the realization that Joseph was still alive and all of the potential ramifications of that reality. The Torah tells us, "His brothers could not answer him, for they were dismayed at his presence" (Genesis 45:3). Rather than beginning as a joyous family reunion of estranged brothers, their reunion with Joseph was initially infused with terror. What would he do? Would they all be sold into slavery for the rest of their lives? Or would they simply be killed for their cold-hearted betrayal of their younger brother? Simeon and Levi quickly glanced at one another as guilt and remorse flooded over them.

At that moment, the cards were definitely not stacked in their favor, so they immediately braced themselves for the full impact of the wrath of Joseph. But it never came. He probably even had to repeat himself: "Is my father still alive?" Judah blinked. Reuben gasped. Gad exhaled deeply. Benjamin cocked his head in bewilderment as he attempted to process all that had taken place over the last few weeks. "Is my father still alive?" Joseph asked yet another time, with his voice choking and tears in his eyes. They still couldn't answer him. So Joseph began to comfort their fears saying, "I am your brother, Joseph, whom you sold into Egypt. And now do not be distressed or angry with yourselves because you sold me here, for God sent me before you to preserve life" (Genesis 45:4–5).

If it hasn't been obvious, Joseph's response is atypical. He doesn't respond with anger. He doesn't retaliate. He doesn't harbor bitterness toward his brothers for literally "selling him out." He sees everything that happened to him as part of a larger plan that God was weaving together over the many years of his misfortune in order to create something larger and more elaborate than a peaceful life for himself. God was using Joseph throughout his difficult life to accomplish His purposes in the earth, though he did not understand why at the time. His continual comfort, however, was his assurance that ultimately God was good, and He was constantly good, despite the circumstances Joseph found himself in.

The Scriptures tell us "he kissed all his brothers and wept upon them" (Genesis 45:14). Because Joseph's eyes were constantly on God and His gracious sovereignty, he did not look to man as the one who controlled his destiny—or his happiness. Yes, his brothers did something awful to him with ill intent. But he did not let that event be his filter for the rest of his life. His filter was God's goodness. Therefore, his heart could never be bitter toward his brothers. They were merely tools in the hands of God to bring about His greater purposes. In this case, it was the salvation of the world. How could Joseph be bitter about that?

The next time things don't go our way, or we get frustrated, or we are mistreated, let's step outside of ourselves and imitate Joseph. We can either allow someone else to control us, or we can control ourselves. No, we probably won't understand our situation any better, but we can make the choice to overcome our flesh and find comfort in the goodness of our Creator. We can become bitter, or we can become better. The choice is ours.

Parashat Vayechi

GENESIS 47:28-50:26

Can Blessings Be A Hidden Curse?

Parashat Vayechi begins differently than all other parashot. It is the only parashah in the entire Torah that is attached to the previous parashah without any means of additional spacing. Unlike all of the other portions, there is no break between Vayigash and Vayechi in the Torah scroll. Our sages interpret this in a number of ways, as they consider the breaks and spaces in the Torah scroll to be equally as important as the letters, and for good reason. Since the spaces within the Torah are used to serve specific functions, there must be a lesson in this peculiarity within the Torah.

One interpretation of this anomaly is that the lack of space between this portion and the previous one is supposed to teach us something about Jacob's children. Rashi proposes that once the children of Israel lost their father, the spiritual leader of the emerging nation, their foresight was cut short. Their fate was concealed from them. Their lives were like a snowball rolling downhill, gathering mass and momentum. There was no time to reflect after the death of their father. They lived as if there were no tomorrow, spiraling toward their fate unaware. Each day ran into the next, until they awoke abruptly in the chains of Egyptian slavery.

We have the potential for this to be repeated in one way or another in our lives also. How so? Sometimes life can get away from us. Sometimes we are so caught up in creating a livelihood or getting the kids off to their soccer games that we forget the things that are important. Sometimes we are so distracted by our jobs and "getting ahead" that we lose sight of the things that should be most dear to us.

Therefore, we have a constant reminder to guard against this in the daily Amidah (the pinnacle of any prayer service). We ask the LORD to bless us "for the good." We say, "Bless for us, Hashem our God, this year and every type of produce *for the good*." Why is the expression, "for the good" added to this prayer? Why don't we just ask for blessings in general? Aren't all blessings good? Not necessarily.

Take for instance the successful businessman who prospers wildly, but he never has time for his wife and children. When one's business dealings are "successful," they can often become all-consuming, allowing little to no time for personal pursuits or spiritual endeavors.

Or what about the one who suddenly comes into an enormous amount of money without any previous experience of managing money properly? Statistics show that the vast majority of those who win a large amount of money generally end up broke and worse off than before their windfall within one year. According to these findings, winning the lottery may seem like an incredible blessing, but could end up being a curse.

There is a story told about a man who inherited a prosperous business from his father. However, rather than the business prospering as it did under the leadership of his father, it took a turn for the worse with the son. Concerned and wondering why the business was not succeeding as it did for his father, he approached his rabbi to get his advice. After relating his predicament to his rabbi, his rabbi asked him, "When business is slow, what do you do with your time?" He replied that he read the newspaper and caught up on the latest news.

"That is your problem!" the rabbi insisted. "When your father was running the business he used his free time to study Torah and perform mitzvot! But you just waste away your time. The *yetzer hara* (the evil impulse) used the success of your father's business to try and distract him from his Torah studies. But you are already distracted, so the yetzer hara does not need to overwhelm you with business!"

We need to constantly pray that the steps we take today will lead us in the proper paths tomorrow. We don't want to be obsessed with business success at the cost of our families, or our health, or even our own soul. Yeshua said it this way: "For what does it profit a man to gain the whole world and forfeit his soul?" Will our spiritual eyes be closed and our discernment be cut short to what lies ahead, or will we take our every step with discernment and eyes wide open? May every blessing we receive be "for the good," and not to our detriment.

Chazak! Chazak! V'nitchazeik! **Be strong! Be strong! And may we be strengthened!**

Parashat Shemot

EXODUS 1:1-6:1

Be A Man

Last week we concluded the book of Genesis and this week we have begun the book of Exodus. Up to this point we have been studying a brief history of the world leading up to the emergence of the Children of Israel. Beginning in the book of Exodus, however, we start to learn about how God calls Israel out from among the other nations of the earth to be a bride to himself. From here we will learn about the marriage covenant between God and Israel, and their unique responsibilities in that covenantal relationship. Right now, though, we are learning about how God raised up a single man who would be faithful over the flock of Israel and lead them in the paths of righteousness. This man, of course, was Moses.

After we read of the miraculous incidents surrounding the birth of Moses and how he was taken into Pharaoh's court to be raised there, we are given our first glimpse into the compassion he had for his own people:

> One day, when Moses had grown up, he went out to his people and looked on their burdens, and he saw an Egyptian beating a Hebrew, one of his people. He looked this way and

Parashat Shemot

that, and seeing no one, he struck down the Egyptian and hid him in the sand. (Exodus 2:11–12)

The English Standard translation says that Moses "looked this way and that, and seeing no one," he took action. However, the Hebrew is a little more visual. It says *ki ein ish*—"because there was no man"—he struck down the Egyptian. We can read this two ways. The first way is to say that because no one was watching him, he killed the Egyptian. This seems to be the plain and simple meaning of the text. However, we can also read it to say that because no other man was available to defend the Hebrew slave, Moses rose to the occasion. If we think about this incident in these terms, it will help us understand the words of Hillel the Elder. Hillel taught his disciples, "In a place where there are no men, strive to be a man" (Avot 2:6). Maybe he had in mind the actions of Moses in this incident. Because no other man was there to do what needed to be done, Moses had to become "a man" who would defend his brother.

Leviticus 19:16 literally says, "You shall not stand against the blood of your neighbor." However, it has always been interpreted to mean that we are obligated to defend those who are not capable to defend themselves. This is exactly what Moses did, and most likely an aspect of what Hillel intended in his statement. We are to "be a man" when no one else is willing to be one.

Recently, a terrorist in Israel ran around and stabbed people at random. An Israeli man saw him and took off after him. After a long chase, he was finally able to subdue the terrorist and bring him to justice, but not without receiving knife wounds himself. In an interview after the event, he described how he did not feel that he was a hero, nor were his actions optional. He said that the Torah did not allow him to stand by idly while the blood of his brothers and sisters was being shed. Because of the values he learned in the Torah, he *became* a man who saved the lives of others and brought a heinous reprobate to justice.

Most of us will never be in a situation like this where we are responsible for the lives of others. However, all of us are put into situations routinely that give us an opportunity to forsake complacency and become a man. As the popular expression goes, "Evil triumphs when good men do nothing." If you look to your left and to your right and don't see a man, then your time has come. Be a man rather than merely looking for one.

Parashat Va'era

EXODUS 6:2-9:35

Offer A Better Product

There's a curious series of events that happens when Moshe and Aaron appear before Pharaoh and display the signs and wonders of Hashem to him and his court. The first thing they do is provide him a sign of their authority from Hashem by turning Aaron's staff into a serpent. However, Pharaoh's magicians also turn their staffs into serpents. And after Hashem turns the water of Egypt into blood, the magicians of Egypt replicate this miracle as well. It says, "But the magicians of Egypt did the same by their secret arts" (Exodus 7:22). Throughout the course of Hashem's display of the various miracles, signs, and wonders on Egypt, Pharaoh's magicians periodically replicate these signs. Why? In order to convince Pharaoh that the God of the Hebrews was no more powerful than they were, and thus allow his heart to be hardened against the Children of Israel.

But Rashi has an interesting and thought-provoking take on this. He says that the magicians are doing this to Moshe and Aaron because bringing signs and wonders to Egypt is like "importing straw to Ofrayim, a city full of straw. You are bringing sorcery to Egypt, which is full of sorcery."

Why would anyone want to bring straw to peddle in a town known for its straw? A person that would have the audacity to do

Parashat Va'era

such a thing had better know beyond a shadow of a doubt that his product was ultimately superior to that which was produced in Straw Town. Otherwise he would suffer the humility that would follow.

In other words, Pharaoh and his magicians were telling Moshe and Aaron, "Why are you peddling your magic here in the capital of magic? We know magic when we see it, and the only way we are going to pay attention to you is if your magic is of a far superior quality than our own." Moshe and Aaron had more than magic, but Pharaoh and his magicians didn't know that. For a long while they saw Moshe and Aaron as trying to compete with the magic of Egypt. Only in the end did they realize the difference between their own product and what these two Hebrews were bringing to Egypt. The magicians thought they had power. But when the God of the Hebrews poured out His signs and wonders upon the land of Egypt, they realized anything they could do was only smoke and mirrors compared to His power.

We must bring straw into Straw Town. We must offer a better quality of product. We can look at this in two ways. First, we need to be able to bring the message of the Torah and the Good News of our Messiah to the world in an authentic manner. For example: We commonly hear people giving a secular or humanistic interpretation or examination of Scripture. It ranges from Hollywood to our Presidents to the History Channel to our next door neighbor. However, they need to hear an authentic interpretation that is built on spirituality and truth. Peter tells us that we must "always [be] prepared to make a defense to anyone who asks you for a reason for the hope that is in you; yet do it with gentleness and respect" (1 Peter 3:15). We need to be able to have an answer for the "problematic verses" others claim to be in the Word of God, and do it with gentleness and respect.

Second, a strong segment of the Church knows the Scriptures forward and backward. But they don't understand them in their proper context, and therefore the result of their interpretations is that Scripture ends up contradicting itself. In this respect, we need to bring "straw to Straw Town" by sharing clear and definitive interpretations of the Holy Scriptures with our brothers and sisters in Yeshua in a genuinely loving manner in order to clear up many Scriptural misunderstandings. The Torah has not been abolished. The commandments have not been set aside (even the "ceremonial" ones). Neither has God's covenant with Israel been, nor His covenant with the Aaronic priesthood. As we know, these are merely misunderstandings of the Scriptures that have been perpetuated over many centuries. But they have the force of longevity behind them. Because they have existed for so long, they have the weight of truth in the minds of most Believers. The only way to overcome these misunderstandings is to be able to present our case in a clear, understandable manner, seasoned with a heavy dose of gentleness, patience, humility, and respect.

The sentiment is changing, but we need more workers in the vineyards. You've got the straw that Straw Town needs. Are you brave enough to share it with them?

Parashat Bo

EXODUS 10:1-13:16

From Generation To Generation

With the opening words of our parashah we hear the very heart of God:

> Then the LORD said to Moses, "Go in to Pharaoh, for I have hardened his heart and the heart of his servants, that I may show these signs of mine among them, and that you may tell in the hearing of your son and of your grandson how I have dealt harshly with the Egyptians and what signs I have done among them, that you may know that I am the LORD." (Exodus 10:1–2)

The entire reason for the battle with Pharaoh is that He wants to create a legacy, a memorial, and a devotion to Himself that will be passed on from generation to generation among the Children of Israel. He says it is so that "you may tell in the hearing of your son and of your grandson." His desire is that the Children of Israel would attach themselves to Him forever, and that there would not be a generation in which He is forgotten. It is therefore the responsibility of parents to teach their children the ways of the LORD, and recount everything He has done in our lives so that they can see His love, His

Parashat Bo

faithfulness, and His greatness.

When Pharaoh momentarily relents after the plague of locusts, he asks Moses whom he intends to take out to the wilderness. Moses replies, "We will go with our young and our old. We will go with our sons and daughters" (Exodus 10:9). Pharaoh snapped back, "The LORD [will indeed] be with you if ever I let you and your little ones go!" (v. 10). The world does not want us to teach our children to serve the LORD. Secular society would like nothing better than for our children to forsake their spiritual heritage. As noted in his biography of Rabbi Menachem Mendel Schneerson (the "Rebbe" of blessed memory, and the seventh leader of Chabad), Joseph Telushkin shows that the Rebbe understood this probably more than anyone.

In a private meeting with a philosophy major, the Rebbe spoke critically of Platonic philosophy on a subject that has rarely been addressed. According to Plato, the family unit is a primary problem of society. Plato believed that children should be stripped from their families and raised by the state without any knowledge of their parents. This would allow them to be "programmed" properly by the state to be dutiful citizens who were loyal to the state above their families. The Rebbe considered this philosophy to be "cruel," and rightly so.

This very thing does happen, however, in communist countries. And it's happening more frequently in our own country. Although we don't live under Pharaoh, we do see his spiritual equivalent in a humanistic attitude in our government and especially our educational system. Pharaoh does not want us to go "with our children." He's fine with us leaving on our own, but he wants to keep the children for himself. He knows if he can raise the children, then he can rule the world. This is why we must do everything within our power to share our spiritual journey "with our sons and daughters."

It can't be a private matter. We can't just practice our faith and expect our children to catch it. We have to continually strive to bring them along with us—not through coercion or force, but through consistency, integrity, and inspiration. We want our children to pass on a legacy of faith to their children and grandchildren as well. The best way we can ensure this continuance is by investing into our children now. We can't leave them with Pharaoh. We have to take them with us.

Parashat Beshalach

EXODUS 13:17-17:16

Don't Pray. Just obey.

In the beginning of our Torah portion, the Children of Israel are faced with a dilemma. Pharaoh realized what a terrible loss he had incurred by allowing the Israelites to leave Egypt, so he begins pursuing them with a massive army. When he and his army catch up with the Children of Israel, they are in a particularly strategic position: they have the Israelites cornered. There is nowhere to go but into the sea. The Torah records the reaction of the Israelites:

> When Pharaoh drew near, the people of Israel lifted up their eyes, and behold, the Egyptians were marching after them, and they feared greatly. And the people of Israel cried out to the LORD. (Exodus 14:10)

The Children of Israel were trapped and they cried out to the LORD. And although the text isn't explicit, it appears that Moses follows their lead:

> The LORD said to Moses, "Why do you cry to me? Tell the people of Israel to go forward. (Exodus 14:15)

Parashat Beshalach

What? Why does Hashem rebuke Moses because he prayed? Isn't this the response God desires? Aren't we supposed to pray about everything, and before doing anything? Doesn't He want us to seek Him in times like these? Isn't this the very purpose of prayer? Rabbi Yehudah recognized the problem most people would associate with this passage and therefore explained the situation:

> At that time, Moses was prolonging his prayer. The Holy One, Blessed be He, said to him: My beloved ones are drowning in the sea and you prolong your prayer to me? Moses said before Him, "Master of the Universe, but what can I do?" God said to him, "Speak to the children of Israel that they go forward. And you, lift up your rod and stretch out your hand" [Exodus 14:15-16]. (Sotah 37a)

In other words, Moses doesn't need to spend time praying about the situation when he could use that time to do what Hashem has already instructed him to do. The Apostle John says something similar:

> If anyone sees his brother committing a sin not leading to death, he shall ask, and God will give him life—to those who commit sins that do not lead to death. There is sin that leads to death; I do not say that one should pray for that. All wrongdoing is sin, but there is sin that does not lead to death. (1 John 5:16–17)

John tells his disciples, "There is sin that leads to death; I do not say that one should pray for that." In other words, if we know that a certain person is struggling in a minor sin we should pray for him. However, if a person is involved in a serious sin that leads to death, we don't need to waste our time praying for him, but should intervene in order to save him from destruction.

James, the brother of our Master, extends this principle to our daily choices as well. He says, "So whoever knows the right thing to do and fails to do it, for him it is sin" (James 4:17). Some people who have followed Yeshua their entire lives still don't understand this point. We don't need to pray about the things God has already told us to do, particularly the things He has told us in His Word. If we are continually praying about what to do when God has already given us His instructions, then we are wasting both our time and His. So if you're in a situation that requires action and the right response has already been give to you through the Scriptures or godly counsel … don't pray. Just obey.

Parashat Yitro

EXODUS 18:1-20:23[26]

Heed The Messenger

This week's parashah is one of the most pivotal in terms of human history. In this parashah, the Creator of the Universe reveals Himself in a manner previously unknown to mankind. It is the pinnacle of the Exodus, and the very reason He delivered His people from Egypt. Hashem delivered the Children of Israel from the bondage of Pharaoh in order to bring them to this moment. It was on Mount Sinai that the LORD called Moses and commissioned him to lead the Children of Israel out of Egypt. And now it was from Sinai that God would reveal Himself and His divine will to His people. His voice would be heard for the first time by an entire people. And for the first time He would call an entire people to Himself as a nation that would be set apart from all other nations on the face of the earth.

But in order for all of this to happen, Hashem had to set the stage to allow His people to hear His voice and accept the offer He would present to them. The specific thing He had to do for this to happen was to get the Israelites to trust in His messenger, his *shaliach*. Therefore, the LORD did great and mighty works through the hand of Moses so that they would fully realize he was indeed sent by Hashem:

Parashat Yitro

> Israel saw the great power that the LORD used against the Egyptians, so the people feared the LORD, and they believed in the LORD and in his servant Moses. (Exodus 14:31)

As the Israelites encamped at the base of Mount Sinai, the mountain was surrounded by various displays of the Divine Presence. Why? Because the LORD needed to remind the people to trust in His shaliach. He explained this to Moses:

> Behold, I am coming to you in a thick cloud, that the people may hear when I speak with you, and may also believe in you forever. (Exodus 19:9)

Believe in Moses forever? But isn't it Yeshua that we are supposed to believe in forever? In his Parable of Lazarus and the Rich Man (Luke 16), Yeshua demonstrates that belief in Moses is not optional, but foundational. In the parable, both Lazarus and a rich man die and enter the realm of the dead. Abraham attends to the needs of Lazarus while the rich man suffers torment. As the rich man is suffering, he begs Abraham to send Lazarus back from the dead to call his brothers to repentance. Abraham responds by telling him, "They have Moses and the Prophets; let them hear them." Immediately the rich man objects, saying, "No, father Abraham, but if someone goes to them from the dead, they will repent." Abraham's response is striking: "If they do not hear Moses and the Prophets, neither will they be convinced if someone should rise from the dead."

Why was faith in Moses so critical for the Children of Israel fleeing Egypt? Because he was the one sent to guide them to their destination and facilitate God's covenant with them. Why has faith in Moses been critical for the Children of Israel since the Exodus?

Because he points them back to that covenant God made with them, reminding them of their responsibility to remain faithful to their Redeemer. Sometimes, however, we forget that our faith in Yeshua should also serve the same purpose. Yeshua's job was to point us back to his Father and his Father's covenant. Each self-disclosure of Hashem required that humanity might believe in His shaliach, but not for the sake of believing in him alone. They were to trust in His shaliach so that, ultimately, they might see beyond the messenger to the One whom the messenger represents, and then hear His voice fresh and anew. Yeshua desired that the world believe in him so that they could ultimately hear the voice of his Father and be united for His purposes:

> That they may all be one, just as you, Father, are in me, and I in you, that they also may be in us, so that the world may believe that you have sent me. (John 17:20–21)

Once we believe in the messenger, we can hear his message. The message of Moses was, "I am giving you a covenant with the Creator of the Universe. Cling to its details—loving God and others through the details of this covenant—and you will live." Yeshua's message was, "Repent—turn back to the covenant of your forefathers—because if you do, the Messianic Kingdom will come upon you." We must do more than believe in the messenger. We must hear his voice and be obedient to his message as well.

Parashat Mishpatim

EXODUS 21:1-24:18

Acting On Behalf Of God

Although Parashat Mishpatim is just over three chapters in length, it contains over fifty of the six hundred and thirteen commandments. It is densely packed with various commandments, particularly those involving civil issues. There's a problem, however, with the application of these commandments if we are attempting to follow a literal reading of the text. Here is an example:

> For every breach of trust, whether it is for an ox, for a donkey, for a sheep, for a cloak, or for any kind of lost thing, of which one says, 'This is it,' the case of both parties shall come before God. The one whom God condemns shall pay double to his neighbor. (Exodus 22:9)

A literal reading of this passage poses numerous problems. How do disputing parties "come before God"? Where is this to take place? Also, according to this passage, "the one whom God condemns" is liable to the financial penalty. But how do they know the verdict? What if both parties believe that God has judged in their favor? How is this resolved?

The problems with this passage revolve around translation. In this passage, both parties are to be brought before אלהים, *elohim*. The problem is that this Hebrew word has a wide variety of meanings. It literally means *god(s)*, but can also mean *God, powers, judges, mighty ones*, etc. Although it is used frequently throughout the Hebrew Scriptures to refer to the Creator, it has numerous other uses. For example, consider Psalm 82:

> God has taken his place in the divine council; in the midst of the gods he holds judgment: How long will you judge unjustly and show partiality to the wicked? Selah. (vv. 1–2)

Who is this divine council? Who are the "gods" among whom the Creator sits to hold judgment? These are the judges of Israel. Only they are able to judge with both justice and injustice and show partiality to the wicked. The angelic host is incapable of injustice and is therefore not being referred to in this passage. These judges are admonished, "Give justice to the weak and the fatherless; maintain the right of the afflicted and the destitute. Rescue the weak and the needy; deliver them from the hand of the wicked" (vv. 3–4). God is rebuking the judges of Israel for failure to deliver true justice.

Just a few verses later, God tells them, "You are gods (*elohim*), sons of the Most High, all of you; nevertheless, like men you shall die, and fall like any prince" (vv. 6–7). This is the passage Yeshua quotes when defending his claim to be the Son of God in John 10:

> Jesus answered them, "Is it not written in your Law, 'I said, you are gods'? If he called them gods to whom the word of God came—and Scripture cannot be broken—do you say of him whom the Father consecrated and sent into the world,

'You are blaspheming,' because I said, 'I am the Son of God'?"
(John 10:34–36)

Yeshua uses this argument to show that just as God has called the judges of Israel by His own designation of "elohim" in Psalm 82 because they act on His behalf, his accusers should not be upset with his claim to be the Son of God, since he was acting with full authority from his Father.

In Parashat Mishpatim, we hear God conferring full authority upon His representatives to make rulings among the Children of Israel on His behalf. The Amplified Bible renders this in a way to help us understand. The Children of Israel are to "bring him to God [that is, to the judges who act in God's name]" (Exodus 22:9, Amplified Bible). The only way a case can be settled is through a system of judges that has authority to interpret Torah and make judgments for Israel.

Yeshua also confers this authority to his Apostles, saying, "Truly, I say to you, whatever you bind on earth shall be bound in heaven, and whatever you loose on earth shall be loosed in heaven" (Matthew 18:18). In each case, the authority acts on behalf of the issuer of that authority. Parashat Mishpatim is filled with a number of cases in which those authorities would need to mediate between the involved parties. Through His agents, God extends Himself into the realm of mankind through righteousness and justice.

Parashat Terumah

EXODUS 25:1-27:19

The Bridge

Up until Parashat Terumah we hear nothing mentioned about a plan to build a Mishkan, a Tabernacle. God had delivered the Children of Israel from Egypt, taken them to be his *Am Segulah* (Treasured People), and given them His Torah. It seemed like a finished product, with the exception of taking them to their land. Now, however, Moses comes back down Mt. Sinai and begins communicating the plans Hashem has given him to build a portable structure that they would set up and tear down at each of their encampments. The Mishkan would become a holy edifice that would allow interaction between God and man. It would be something like a portal by which the priesthood would be able to enter the presence of the Almighty, similar to what only Moses was allowed to do thus far. But in order to accomplish this momentous task, the Children of Israel would have to work together for this common cause. The Torah records for us Hashem's request:

> The LORD said to Moses, "Speak to the people of Israel, that they take for me a contribution. From every man whose heart moves him you shall receive the contribution for me." (Exodus 25:1–2)

What was the goal? Was it so that God could dwell in a structure? Was it so that they could rival pagan religious practices? No. He gives Moses the reason. He said, "And let them make me a sanctuary, that I may dwell in their midst" (Exodus 25:8). Hashem desired the Tabernacle to be built for this single reason. He wanted to create a bridge between God and man, an edifice that could cross over both time and space to bring man into union with his Creator. But in order for this structure to fulfill its purpose, it couldn't be just a structure. It had to be built in such a way that it was a miniature copy of the Divine Tabernacle that already existed in the heavenly realm. Hashem told Moses:

> Exactly as I show you concerning the pattern of the tabernacle, and of all its furniture, so you shall make it.
> (Exodus 25:9)

The author of the book of Hebrews emphasizes this point by saying that the Tabernacle was created to "serve as a copy and shadow of the heavenly things" (Hebrews 8:5). It was to be the closest thing on earth to the dwelling place of God in Heaven. Its sanctity (holiness) was unparalleled.

But this sanctity could not exist without boundaries. Holiness can exist only within boundaries, because holiness is defined in terms of boundaries. The Tabernacle proper (and all of its furnishings) was strictly off limits to the common Israelite. Only the Levites were allowed access to this holy house, and even they were limited in their access. Portions of it were accessible only by the Kohanim, the priesthood. But if the idea of the Tabernacle was to be a bridge between God and man, then why was access to it restricted to a select group of people? Shouldn't it have been freely accessible to everyone?

In a marriage, intimacy is not achieved through allowing others equal access to our spouses. Intimacy is achieved only through establishing the proper boundaries in order to protect the relationship between a man and his wife. In a healthy marriage, no one else should occupy the space in our hearts reserved only for our spouse. This is a protection against infidelity. Why does the Ark of the Covenant alone rest at the heart of the Tabernacle? Because it contained the covenant—the boundaries—that allowed for God's intimacy with man. True intimacy exists within boundaries.

The world wants us to believe that boundaries are barriers to intimacy. And unfortunately, a large majority of the church has fallen for this line of reasoning as well. However, rather than barriers, those boundaries are what undergird holiness and intimacy. The Tabernacle established boundaries for the Children of Israel, but only for the purpose of becoming a bridge by which they could encounter the God of the Universe. The Torah establishes boundaries between common man and a holy God. We can view it as either a barrier or a bridge. Which one do you see it as?

Parashat Tetzaveh

EXODUS 27:20-30:10

The Beauty Of Boundaries

After giving instructions for making the oil for the Temple menorah, Parashat Tetzaveh is primarily focused on the consecration of the *kohanim* (priests). This consecration includes how the priestly garments, particularly those of the *Kohen Gadol* (high priest), were to be tailored. The garments of the Kohan Gadol were to be unique in every way. One garment in particular, the ephod, was to be made of a special combination of various materials:

> And they shall make the ephod of gold, of blue and purple and scarlet yarns, and of fine twined linen, skillfully worked. (Exodus 28:6)

These components—gold thread, blue yarn, purple yarn, scarlet yarn, and fine linen—were all to be woven together by an expert craftsman to create something beautiful and unique for the man who would serve in the most holy position on earth. Since the gold was to be used as in the fabric itself, creating this gold thread would have been a challenging endeavor. The blue, purple, and scarlet yarn would have been made from the wool of sheep or goats that had been dyed to a rich and vibrant color. The linen (made from the fibers of flax stalks), however, would have been either left in its natural color or bleached to appear a pure white. Once all of these materials were woven together, the ephod would have taken on a color, texture, and pattern that would set the Kohen Gadol apart from all of the other kohanim designated to serve Hashem.

A problem arises, however, when we get to a prohibition recorded for us in Deuteronomy. It says, "You shall not wear cloth of wool and linen mixed together" (Deuteronomy 22:11). According to the Torah, wool and linen are not permitted to be woven together. So how does this apply to the garments of the Kohen Gadol? In situations like this, we apply the principle in the Talmud taught to us by Reish Lakish: "Any place where you find a positive mitzva and a prohibition that clash with one another, if you can find some way to fulfill both, that is preferable; and if that is not possible, the positive mitzva will come and override the prohibition" (b.Nazir 41a). Therefore, the positive commandment to blend the fibers to create the ephod for the Kohen Gadol overrides the general prohibition of not mixing wool and linen together.

Why then does the Torah prohibit the mixture of wool and linen to begin with? Is there a chemical or physical reaction that takes place between the wool and the linen? Possibly, but that is not likely the reason for this prohibition. Most likely this prohibition involves boundaries of distinction between the Kohen Gadol and everyone else. Hashem has designated him as the most holy man on the face of the earth. But if the common Israelite, or even the other kohanim, are able to wear garments that are similar or the same as his, then his holiness—his set-apartness—is diminished. This is also why the Torah prohibits the replication of the incense that is to be used in the Tent of Meeting. To replicate it and use it for purposes outside of the context of the holy service is to profane it and make it common.

Many times we innocently attempt to replicate what we see in the beauty of something that was intended to be holy and distinct. However, as we have noted, when lines of distinction are blurred, holiness is lost. In order for something to remain holy, it cannot become common. Peter applied this principle to living a life that is holy:

> As obedient children, do not be conformed to the passions of your former ignorance, but as he who called you is holy, you also be holy in all your conduct, since it is written, "You shall be holy, for I am holy." (1 Peter 1:14–16)

When we try to bring holiness down to our level, then holiness is lost. But it is also lost when we don't live up to the level of holiness that is expected of us. Holiness is being unique and set apart. Disciples of Yeshua should reflect the appropriate measure of holiness in our lives.

Parashat Ki Tisa

EXODUS 30:11–34:35

Your Rules or Mine?

For the last few Torah portions, we have been reading and learning about the construction of the Tabernacle and everything that needed to be done for it to function properly. Over the last several chapters, Hashem has been dictating to Moses the exact instructions for the Tabernacle and its furnishings, as well as the garments for the *kohanim* (priests). This week's parashah concludes these instructions. However, immediately upon giving the last instruction regarding who was to be in charge of all of the craftsmanship, Hashem gives the Children of Israel a stern and detailed warning that none of these things were to be done on Shabbat:

> Speak to the Israelite people and say: Nevertheless, you must keep My sabbaths, for this is a sign between Me and you throughout the ages, that you may know that I the LORD have consecrated you. You shall keep the sabbath, for it is holy for you. He who profanes it shall be put to death: whoever does work on it, that person shall be cut off from among his kin. Six days may work be done, but on the seventh day there shall be a sabbath of complete rest, holy to the LORD; whoever does work on the sabbath day shall

> be put to death. The Israelite people shall keep the sabbath, observing the sabbath throughout the ages as a covenant for all time: it shall be a sign for all time between Me and the people of Israel. For in six days the LORD made heaven and earth, and on the seventh day He ceased from work and was refreshed. (Exodus 31:12–17)

This admonition is the first time we learn of the severe consequences of breaking the Sabbath. Willful transgression of the Sabbath day while living within a theocratic, Torah-based community results in the death penalty.

But what constitutes a Sabbath violation? If violating the Sabbath will result in the dire consequence of the death penalty, then surely the parameters of violating the Sabbath are clearly spelled out in the Torah, right? However, a thorough examination of the entire Torah will not be able to produce any kind of list defining the parameters of what it means to "profane the sabbath," outside of two instances. The first is to not kindle a fire (Exodus 35:3), and the second has something to do with gathering sticks (Numbers 15:32–36). But even these are far from being explicit. For example, what constitutes kindling? Is it how the fire is initially created, or does it have something to do with adding fuel to an existing flame? And what is this business about gathering sticks? What's so wrong with this, and why did a man have to lose his life over it?

Because the consequence of this offense was so serious and the guidelines in the Torah are so ambiguous, Israel had to have a clear means by which capital cases that involved Sabbath violations could be adjudicated. There had to be a clear legal definition of what it meant to either keep the Sabbath or break the Sabbath. Therefore, since this passage is the first mention of the death penalty in relationship to the Sabbath, the judges of Israel determined to use this passage as the precedent for determining the boundaries of the Sabbath. Since Hashem gave the explicit command to not engage in these activities on the Sabbath, even for the construction of the Tabernacle, the various labors that were needed to build the Tabernacle and its furnishings were used as the guidelines for determining what must not be done on the Sabbath. Therefore, a total of thirty-nine categories of prohibitions became the legally defined boundaries of what it means to desecrate the Sabbath, and is recorded for us in the Mishnah (the codification of Jewish law).

Sometimes it's very tempting to define what the Torah means on our own terms. But whose definition is binding? Do we play by your rules or mine? We must always remember that the Torah was given to a nation, not to individuals. While we may have our own interpretations, we do not have any legal authority to say our interpretation is binding. Only the judges of Israel have that authority, and the parameters for how Sabbath must be guarded were established a very long time ago by that authority.

Parashat Vayakhel

EXODUS 35:1-38:20

Kindling A Fire

In most years, Parashat Vayakhel and Parashat Pekudei are read together to conclude the book of Shemot (Exodus). When many people read these parashot, they seem to experience a sense of déjà vu. "Didn't we read about this already?" they might ask. This is because these portions run nearly parallel to the earlier portions of Terumah and Tetzaveh, and even to Ki Tisa. Whereas the previous parashot detailed Hashem's instruction to Moses about the preparations needed for the service of the Tabernacle, this week's portion begins the process of Moses conveying this information to the Children of Israel and beginning the actual work. Therefore, there is a lot of overlap and repetition from previous portions in both Vayakhel and Pekudei.

One thing, however, is unique to Parashat Vayakhel. As we recall from Parashat Ki Tisa, Hashem gave Moses clear instructions that, although He was giving the Children the monumental task of constructing a Tabernacle for His Presence, none of the labors used in the construction of the Tabernacle was permitted to be done on Shabbat. However, our current parashah includes a detail about these prohibitions that we did not see in our previous parashah. At the beginning of our portion, Moses instructs the Children of Israel:

"You shall kindle no fire in all your dwelling places on the Sabbath day." (Exodus 35:3)

When we read this, a question should immediately come to mind: Where did this instruction come from? It is not mentioned in Hashem's previous instructions to Moses. It seems like Moses pulled it out of the air. Did he "add" to what Hashem had said? And to further complicate matters, of all the Sabbath restrictions detailed in Jewish law, this is the only one that is explicitly stated in the entire Torah. Why is this, and what can we learn from it?

First, we should remember that every word of the Torah is of Divine origin. That being the case, even if Moses did add the command to the instructions he received, it was under the direct inspiration of the Holy Spirit and therefore by the permission of Hashem. We should not consider this commandment to be outside the scope of being authoritative in any way. As we will see shortly, this commandment was already in place in some form several chapters earlier.

Next, we can learn at least two lessons from this commandment. The first lesson comes from the *pashat*, or face-value, interpretation. Kindling a fire on Shabbat is a serious offense, and it should be stated clearly that doing so will elicit a harsh punishment from the hands of Heaven. This prohibition includes using fire in any constructive manner, including cooking. This is why Moses previously told the Children of Israel, "Tomorrow is a day of solemn rest, a holy Sabbath to the Lord; bake what you will bake and boil what you will boil, and all that is left over lay aside to be kept till the morning" (Exodus 16:23). Since fire could not be used for cooking on Shabbat, all of the cooking had to be done ahead of time. This is still the rule today.

The second lesson we can learn comes from the *derash*, or homiletic, interpretation. Fire is frequently associated with anger, as it is written:

> Therefore, when the LORD heard, he was full of wrath; a fire was kindled against Jacob; his anger rose against Israel.
> (Psalm 78:21)

As seen in this example, arousing one's anger can homiletically be considered "kindling a fire." The Sabbath is a time for shalom—peace, tranquility, wholeness. To arouse anger in oneself or in another person is not fitting for the Sabbath. Anger is not an appropriate response in most instances during the week anyway, so avoiding the arousal of this destructive force so as not to disrupt the sanctity of Shabbat is even more important. We always keep in mind that we should never act in a manner that would allow the flame of anger to be kindled on the holy day of Shabbat. By remembering this and putting it into practice, the Sabbath Queen will be welcome in our homes and the Light of Messiah will shine in our midst.

Parashat Pekudei

EXODUS 38:21-40:38

The Blessing of Obedience

Parashat Pekudei is the concluding parashah of the book of Shemot, Exodus. For the last several weeks we have been studying about all of the various instructions for building the Tabernacle and its furnishings, the details of how the priestly garments were to be made, and how the services of the Tabernacle should function. In our current parashah, however, we see the work completed and the Tabernacle inaugurated.

Our portion begins by reminding us that all of the materials for the Tabernacle and its service were created by Bezalel, Ohaliab, and their team of artisans. After this, we are given the details regarding the creation of the priestly garments, which ends the list of items that were made for the service of the Tabernacle. Throughout this section, a common phrase is frequently repeated: *ka'asher tzivah Hashem et Moshe*—according to all that the LORD commanded Moses. As we know, when the Torah repeats a phrase, we should take note. We should realize that it is emphasizing something important to us. Indeed, it is the case in this situation as well, because at the conclusion of this section we read:

Parashat Pekudei

> According to all that the LORD had commanded Moses, so the people of Israel had done all the work. And Moses saw all the work, and behold, they had done it; as the LORD had commanded, so had they done it. Then Moses blessed them. (Exodus 39:42–43)

On the first day of Nissan, a full year from their departure from Egypt, all of the materials were brought to Moses so that he could oversee its assembly. Because Bezalel, Ohaliab, and their team of artisans followed Hashem's instructions meticulously and carried out all of the work with great detail and accuracy, the Torah makes note of this. It says that when their job was complete, "Moses blessed them." Although a blessing from Moses would surely have been an incredible experience, the story doesn't end there. When the Tabernacle was assembled piece by piece and its furnishings placed inside, something incredible happened:

> Then the cloud covered the tent of meeting, and the glory of the LORD filled the tabernacle. And Moses was not able to enter the tent of meeting because the cloud settled on it, and the glory of the LORD filled the tabernacle. (Exodus 40:34–35)

Unlike the construction of most things today, the Children of Israel didn't have any pieces left over when they were finished, nor did they lack any. They had followed the instructions exactly as they had received them. Therefore, when they had completed their work and the Tabernacle was assembled, it was perfect. The presence of Hashem took up residence among the sons of men in the form of a cloud, and the "glory of the LORD" was manifested in the Holy

House—so much so that Moses could not even enter into the structure. This sign from Heaven was Hashem's approval of the work of the Children of Israel, assuring them that He was pleased with their work and His presence would go with them on their journey.

From this example we can see that the Children of Israel were blessed with the presence of the LORD because of their obedience. Obedience brings blessing and the presence of Hashem. Paul emphasized this principle to the believers in Rome:

> Do you not know that if you present yourselves to anyone as obedient slaves, you are slaves of the one whom you obey, either of sin, which leads to death, or of obedience, which leads to righteousness? But thanks be to God, that you who were once slaves of sin have become obedient from the heart to the standard of teaching to which you were committed, and, having been set free from sin, have become slaves of righteousness. (Romans 6:16–18)

We cannot expect blessings and God's presence when we are living in disobedience. If the Children of Israel had not constructed the Tabernacle and all of its furnishings according to all of the details given to Moses, then Hashem's presence would not have been able to dwell in their midst.

We have a similar opportunity. We have the opportunity to usher the presence of the Almighty into this world every single day through living a life of obedience. Will it be like it was in the days of the Tabernacle? Probably not. However, it will definitely make an impact on those around us. The bottom line is this: We can choose to be slaves to sin or slaves to righteousness. If we choose to remain slaves to sin, we are no better off than before we were redeemed.

However, by choosing to be slaves to righteousness, we have the potential to bring redemption to this world. May we all merit the return of our Master Yeshua and the establishment of his Kingdom on earth through our obedience to Hashem and our devotion to His Messiah. Maranatha!

Chazak! Chazak! V'nitchazeik! **Be strong! Be strong! And may we be strengthened!**

Parashat Vayikra

LEVITICUS 1:1-5:26[6:7]

Drawing Near: On Whose Terms?

As we finish the book of Shemot (Exodus), we now turn to the book of Vayikra (Leviticus). When most people begin a study of the book of Leviticus, they probably don't get that excited. It's focused almost entirely on animal sacrifices, various sprinklings of blood, bodily discharges, and purification rituals. The modern reader finds a study of Leviticus more repulsive than edifying. This is because these rituals are foreign to the modern reader in a time when animal sacrifice is considered more barbaric than spiritual.

But in the days of the Master, these issues would have been extremely relevant to those wanting to draw near to the God of Abraham, Isaac, and Jacob. Their significance would not have been lost, nor reduced to "types and shadows" as they are often understood today. For Israelites living in a time when the Holy Temple in Jerusalem stood, sacrifices and purification rituals occupied sacred space. This tradition, however, was not of their own design, but originated from their Redeemer.

They learned this from a very early age. At the age of five, Jewish children begin their Torah studies with the book of Leviticus. Why Leviticus? The midrash explains:

Parashat Vayikra

> Why do young children commence with The Law of the Priests (i.e. Leviticus), and not with Genesis? Surely it is because young children are pure, and the sacrifices are pure; so let the pure come and engage in the study of the pure. (Midrash Rabbah 7:3)

Paul makes a similar statement in his instruction to Titus that might help us understand this concept:

> To the pure, all things are pure, but to the defiled and unbelieving, nothing is pure; but both their minds and their consciences are defiled. (Titus 1:15)

In Hebrew, the overarching term for any kind of offering is the word *korban*. Given the typical understanding of sacrifices, one would think that this word is derived from the concepts of extravagant giving, self-deprivation, or even self-annulment. However, the word korban comes from the word *karav*, which means to draw near. A korban, a sacrifice, is something given to draw near to God. However, we are not to give Him whatever we feel like. We are to give Him what He has asked for.

Consider this. A young man asks his newlywed wife what he can get for her. She says she would love a bouquet of fresh flowers. Being very practical, the young man begins to reason that this is not a wise choice. After all, flowers will last only a few days and then be thrown into the trash. He should give his worthy bride something with more longevity like a vacuum cleaner or a toaster. But will this fulfill the desire of his bride? Of course not. His "thoughtful" gift may even end up being a source of contention.

This is why the prophet Samuel can chastise King Saul for his lavish sacrificial offerings by saying, "Behold, to obey is better than sacrifice, and to listen than the fat of rams" (1 Samuel 15:22). Saul had missed the concept of sacrifice entirely. He tried to approach God on his own terms. He believed that giving Hashem the choicest selections from his spoils would negate his disobedience. He tried to use his sacrifices to assuage God's anger, rather than for their intended purpose of drawing closer to Him. His disobedience created distance from Hashem that his korbanot could not reconcile.

True love will love a person in the way they need to be loved, rather than the way we think they should be loved. Too many times we try to approach Hashem on our own terms. The sacrificial system is Hashem's love language. By studying the laws of the korbanot in Leviticus, we draw near to God in a way that is on His terms rather than our own. Why not spend a little extra time learning about their details so that we can draw close to our God?

Parashat Tzav
LEVITICUS 6:1[8]-8:36

Keep The Fire Burning

In our second week of learning about the sacrificial system, we read about the laws of what is known as the *korban tamid*, or the daily offering. Our portion begins by telling us, "This is the law of the burnt offering" (Leviticus 6:2[9]). The burnt offerings in this passage are not voluntary burnt offerings brought by petitioners, but rather the continual (*tamid*) or daily offerings required to be brought at the beginning and end of every single day: "One lamb you shall offer in the morning, and the other lamb you shall offer toward the evening" (Exodus 29:39). These two offerings serve as bookends to the daily services of the Holy House. They also serve as the basis for the daily prayer times. The morning prayers (*shacharit*) and the afternoon prayers (*minchah*) correspond to these two daily offerings.

When discussing these particular *korbanot* (offerings), the Torah specifies that the fire that burns on the altar should never be allowed to be extinguished. It emphasizes this point three times in our portion:

> The fire of the altar shall be kept burning on it. (Leviticus 6:2[9])

Parashat Tzav

> The fire on the altar shall be kept burning on it. (Leviticus 6:5[12])

> Fire shall be kept burning on the altar continually; it shall not go out. (Leviticus 6:6[13])

From this repetition we learn that at least three separate fires were burning on the altar in different locations: one for burning the offerings, one for the coals required to be used while burning the incense on the Golden Altar, and one simply to ensure that a continual flame remained on the altar in the event the others should ever fail. This last one is where we will focus our attention.

We can derive a few applications from this command to keep the fire ablaze upon the altar. The first is the literal understanding. When there is a functioning Temple, the fire on the altar must never go out. It must be tended to and stoked so that the flame of the altar will never be extinguished. The second application is that during a time when the Holy Temple is not functioning, the altar fire should be kept alive through our prayers. Every morning and afternoon during our daily prayers, we recite the laws of the korban tamid that are placed upon the fire of the altar each and every day that the Holy House is functioning. Since we live in a time when the Holy Temple is not functioning, we keep the fire burning metaphorically upon the holy altar through this daily recitation.

The last application is that we must never allow the flame of Torah and mitzvot to be extinguished upon the altar of our hearts. We must continually find ways to keep this flame alive. We must daily strive to increase our Torah learning and how we live out the commandments. Everything we do should point toward the restoration of the Kingdom and the return of our King. However, we should strive to keep the flame of Torah and mitzvot alive within us, and encourage others to as well, because the Day is drawing near:

> And let us consider how to stir up one another to love and good works, not neglecting to meet together, as is the habit of some, but encouraging one another, and all the more as you see the Day drawing near. (Hebrews 10:24–25)

When the disciples of Yeshua encountered him on the road to Emmaus, their hearts burned within them as he taught them Torah. They said, "Did not our hearts burn within us while he talked to us on the road, while he opened to us the Scriptures?" (Luke 24:32). Our hearts should also burn with the words of our rabbi, igniting a flame within us for Torah and mitzvot. However, we cannot expect that flame to last indefinitely without attendance, so we must work diligently to assure its survival. What will you do today to keep the holy fire continually burning on your altar? What will you do to help your brother attend the fire on the altar of his heart as well?

Parashat Shemini

LEVITICUS 9:1-11:47

Searching Diligently

Parashat Shemini covers the inauguration procedures for the service of the Tabernacle, as well as the dietary laws that spell out which animals are fit for consumption. Sandwiched between these topics, we learn about a tragic event that results in the death of two of Aaron's sons, Nadab and Abihu. They attempt to approach Hashem on their own terms by bringing "unauthorized fire" into the presence of the Holy One of Israel. The event that follows is horrific. The Torah tells us, "Fire came out from before the LORD and consumed them, and they died before the LORD" (Leviticus 10:2).

After this tragedy, Moses instructed Aaron, Eleazar, and Ithamar (Aaron's two surviving sons) on the details of eating the various offerings that were used for the service. But when the service was complete, Moses realized that one of the offerings was entirely consumed on the fire instead of eaten. He became angry at Eleazar and Ithamar for not eating it and chastised them for this. Immediately, Aaron responded to his accusations and justified the actions of his sons. Who was right? Aaron or Moses?

Before we look to the answer, we need to understand what Moses did in this situation. Most Bible translations will say something like, "Moses searched diligently" for an answer to this dilemma.

However, the Hebrew is a little more interesting. It uses the phrase, "*darosh darash*." These are two forms of the same Hebrew word, whose root means "to search out." What is even more significant about this phrase describing Moses' intense inquiry is that these two words are believed to be located at the very center—the very heart—of the Torah.

Torah is all about searching and finding. Proverbs tells us, "It is the glory of God to conceal things, but the glory of kings is to search things out" (Proverbs 25:2). Yeshua tells us that we should continually "ask, seek, and knock." The deeper we search, the more treasures we will find. We will always be able to find beautiful things on the surface. However, only when we dig deep will we discover the precious jewels that are waiting to be discovered. We can use this situation as an instance of digging to reveal hidden jewels.

The argument between Moses and Aaron is the first halachic debate we have recorded. The Torah had barely been given, yet there was confusion as to how it should be understood and adhered to. Since Moses was the one God used to teach the Children of Israel His divine Law, and since he had already thoroughly searched out the matter, one would imagine that the instruction of Moses would be the final word in this case. However, in the end, Moses humbly admits that he is in the wrong and that Aaron is the one who has ruled correctly.

We can all learn an important lesson here. Moses searched out the matter thoroughly, but still ended up being wrong. And although he made a wrong decision, it didn't destroy him. He remains the greatest national leader in the history of Israel. Why? Because he was humble, "more than all people who were on the face of the earth" (Numbers 12:3). Moses didn't have an issue with his ego. His humility allowed him to admit when he was wrong and yet still be able to teach and lead others. Rabbi Tzadok taught his disciples, "Do not make the Torah a crown with which to aggrandize yourself, nor use it as a spade with which to dig" (Avot 4:7). Digging deep into the Torah will fill the treasure houses of our hearts. But if we dig only to endorse our dogma, then we have missed the heart of the Torah.

Parashat Tazria
LEVITICUS 12:1-13:59

Spiritual Biohazard

This week's Torah portion discusses two topics largely skipped over by Bible students today: the laws of purification after childbirth, and biblical leprosy. These two topics are a typical cross-section of the various topics covered by the book of Leviticus and why it is largely avoided by even the most serious students of the Scriptures. However, since the LORD considered these topics important enough to populate the Holy Scriptures, we would do well to at least familiarize ourselves with them. Let's take a brief look at the topic of biblical leprosy.

When the Torah speaks of biblical leprosy, we must keep in mind that this is not the same as modern leprosy. Modern leprosy is a bacterial infection also known as Hansen's disease. Although it can be a debilitating disease, it is completely treatable if caught in time. Biblical leprosy, known in the Hebrew Scriptures as *tzara'at*, is not caused by a bacterial or viral infection, and it has no known prescriptive cure. Biblical leprosy affected only one's status of ritual purity and communal participation. Let's take a brief look at tzara'at and a few of its appearances in the Torah.

We have only two recorded instances of tzara'at in the Torah. The first is when Hashem encountered Moses at the burning bush.

Parashat Tazria

Hashem told Moses to put his hand in his cloak, and when he pulled it out the Torah tell us that it was "leprous like snow" (Exodus 4:6). This was the result of Moses' objection to Hashem's instructions to speak to the Children of Israel regarding their salvation. He said, "But behold, they will not believe me or listen to my voice, for they will say, 'The LORD did not appear to you' " (Exodus 4:1). The other occurrence is where Miriam is temporarily stricken with leprosy. The Torah records that Miriam "spoke against Moses because of the Cushite woman whom he had married, for he had married a Cushite woman" (Numbers 12:1). As a result she was stricken with tzara'at for seven days. In both of these instances, the person inflicted was guilty of slander—Moses against the Children of Israel, and Miriam against Moses.

Tzara'at has several unusual characteristics. First, a person who has tzara'at is called a *metzora*. However, when a person had the symptoms of tzara'at, it did not automatically mean they were a metzora. They could be declared a metzora only by the official diagnosis of the priest (see Leviticus 13). Once a person was declared to have biblical leprosy, they were declared ritually unclean and had to remain in isolation outside of the Israelite encampment.

Another unusual characteristic is that if the tzara'at spread to the point at which it covered the entire flesh of the metzora, the priest was to reverse his status and declare him ritually clean (Leviticus 13:17). If this were an infectious disease, such as Hansen's disease, then declaring him ritually clean would be counter-productive and a liability to the community. Surely there is something more going on than meets the eye.

In Hebrew, the word metzora has the same letters as the phrase *motzi [shem] ra*, which means "causing an evil [name or reputation]." From the spelling of the word, as well as these two events recorded in the Torah, our sages connected tzara'at with *lashon hara* (evil speech). Tzara'at was contracted only due to gossip and slander, and was a supernatural disease that was in effect only in a time that the Tabernacle or Temple stood. Tzara'at was not a pathological biohazard as one might think, but a spiritual biohazard. It seems Hashem was extremely concerned about how His children spoke of one another, and He took extreme measures to show the severity of it.

How does this apply for us today? Just because we don't have the outward manifestation of tzara'at today doesn't mean that we can freely slander our brothers and sisters without fear of consequence. Studying the laws of this consequence that Hashem designated for slanderers is a constant reminder that, although we may think we can get by with something that doesn't seem so bad in our eyes, the dignity of another person is always esteemed in the eyes of our Creator. We may not see any consequences today, but one day the books will be opened and our actions revealed for all to see. May we be reminded about the laws of the metzora, and may our speech be pure at all times.

Parashat Metzora

LEVITICUS 14:1–15:33

Approaching The Wholly Holy

On most years, the portions of Tazria and Metzora are read together. Both of these portions primarily detail the laws surrounding *tzara'at*, biblical leprosy. Whereas Parashat Tazria focuses almost entirely on diagnosing tzara'at, Parashat Metzora is concerned more about the purification process after a person has been healed from tzara'at. Our parashah concludes by detailing laws of purity surrounding bodily discharges from both men and women.

When one studies portions like these, it seems that the Torah, particularly the book of Leviticus, focuses disproportionately upon these strange and bizarre determinations and rituals. Who cares about the various colors of a skin malady or the antiquated taboos revolving around bodily functions? Why should anyone trudge through these topics and study them with any detail? The answer to these questions comes at the end of our parashah. Hashem sums up His reason for detailing these rituals:

> Thus you shall keep the people of Israel separate from their uncleanness, lest they die in their uncleanness by defiling my tabernacle that is in their midst. (Leviticus 15:31)

First, the Children of Israel are supposed make a distinction between clean and unclean. It was the responsibility of the Kohanim (priests) to teach these distinctions:

> You are to distinguish between the holy and the common, and between the unclean and the clean, and you are to teach the people of Israel all the statutes that the LORD has spoken to them by Moses. (Leviticus 10:10–11)

The laws of ritual purity were to be clarified by the Kohanim and understood by every Israelite to the best of their ability in order that the Children of Israel not remain in their impurity. Once they became ritually unclean, their responsibility was to go through the prescribed rituals to regain ritual purity. As we have seen, some types of ritual impurity were easier to cleanse than others, with corpse contamination being at the top of the list as the most persistent form of ritual impurity.

Second, failure to understand these distinctions and laws could have catastrophic results. For clarification, issues of ritual purity were generally unrelated to sin and therefore had no immediate ramifications. Nothing is inherently sinful about becoming ritually unclean. Yeshua and the Apostles would have become ritually unclean many times throughout their lives. It was simply a part of life. The problem arises, however, when ritual impurity impinges upon sanctified space. According to God, something is very wrong with this. Bringing ritual impurity into sanctified space is like mixing chlorine with ammonia: it is toxic.

Living in a modern society outside of the land of Israel and in a time when the Holy Temple is not functional, most Bible students cannot grasp the gravity of this concept. How does attending a funeral followed by prayer at the Temple constitute the death penalty? It just doesn't seem reasonable to us, since no visible difference can be distinguished between one event and the next. But we have to remember that the Holy House is the intersection between heaven and earth, between God and man. It is a place unlike any other on the face of the earth. It is the abode of the Holy One, and He established it in order that He might dwell among humans. A holy God cannot abide in profane (common) space. If we remember, every furnishing of the Holy Temple was sanctified and atoned for before it could be used. They had to be purged from the muck of human mortality in order to perform the sacred tasks they were assigned.

Therefore, the laws of ritual purity, as outlined in our recent Torah portions and throughout most of the book of Leviticus, are critical to the proper function of the Holy Temple. Worshippers would have been educated in these passages and well-acquainted with the strictures and penalties of entering God's Holy House in a state of ritual impurity.

What about today? Do these things have a bearing on us today in a time when we don't have access to the Temple? Maybe they should be a reminder of how we come into the Divine Presence in our times of worship. Whether it is communal or personal prayer time, congregational worship, or study of the holy Scriptures, we should seriously consider the state in which we are approaching a God who is wholly holy:

> For thus says the One who is high and lifted up, who inhabits eternity, whose name is Holy: "I dwell in the high and holy place, and also with him who is of a contrite and lowly spirit, to revive the spirit of the lowly, and to revive the heart of the contrite." (Isaiah 57:15)

Parashat Metzora should be a clear reminder that He is not like us. Yes, we are made in His image, but He is not mortal and should not be approached in the same manner as any other being, but on His terms and His terms alone.

Parashat Acharei Mot

LEVITICUS 16:1-18:30

Gateway To Heaven

The portions of Acharei Mot and Kedoshim are read together in non-leap years on the Jewish calendar. These two portions cover a lot of ground in a small amount of space. They cover the ritual of Yom Kippur (Day of Atonement), restrictions on where and how sacrifices can be made, proscriptions for the resident alien, a list of prohibited sexual relations. Needless to say, there is a lot to absorb in this week's dosage of Torah. Let's take a look at one concept associated with Yom Kippur.

The focal point of the Yom Kippur service is the two goats. The first is designated as a sin offering, while the second carries with it the iniquities of the Children of Israel into the wilderness. However, most people are confused as to the purpose of the first goat. It is commonly thought that the sacrifice of this goat designated as a "sin offering" was for the purpose of removing sin from the Children of Israel. And passages in the book of Hebrews alluding to the Yom Kippur service complicate matters even further. However, if we look at the prescription for this goat within the Yom Kippur service, we find that it serves an entirely different purpose:

Parashat Acharei Mot

> Then he shall kill the goat of the sin offering that is for the people and bring its blood inside the veil and do with its blood as he did with the blood of the bull, sprinkling it over the mercy seat and in front of the mercy seat. Thus he shall make atonement for the Holy Place, because of the uncleannesses of the people of Israel and because of their transgressions, all their sins. And so he shall do for the tent of meeting, which dwells with them in the midst of their uncleannesses. (Leviticus 16:15–16)

Rather than being used to cleanse the people from their sins, the blood of the first goat of Yom Kippur was used for the purpose of "atoning for the Holy Place and the tent of meeting and the altar" (v. 20). It was used to remove the contamination of sins from the Tabernacle, the Ark of the Covenant, and the Bronze Altar (vv. 15–19).

The Tabernacle functioned something akin to a bridge or a gateway that served as a link between heaven and earth, allowing for the interaction between God and man, as it is written, "And let them make me a sanctuary, that I may dwell in their midst" (Exodus 25:8). This portal, however, was susceptible to contamination. This corridor between heaven and earth was so important that it had to remain accessible, and therefore it had to be periodically cleansed. Every year the Yom Kippur ritual was performed in order to purge the Tabernacle and its furnishings from the accumulation of the "uncleannesses of the people of Israel" (v. 19), in order that this bridge between God and man not be corrupted.

Since we live in a time when the Holy Temple is not functioning, it is easy to forget about the detailed process of purification undertaken each year to ensure the gateway to heaven would be free from any spiritual debris that might restrict the flow of the Divine

Presence into this world. However, we can carry this reminder into our daily lives. The Apostolic Scriptures portray disciples of Yeshua as miniature temples who house the Spirit of the Most High and carry His presence into the world. Paul reminds the believers at Corinth of this:

> Do you not know that you are God's temple and that God's Spirit dwells in you? ... For God's temple is holy, and you are that temple. (1 Corinthians 3:16–17)

As disciples of Yeshua, we are connecting points between heaven and earth. We can either aid the flow of holiness and godliness in this world, or we can obstruct it. If we allow the muck of the world to cling to us, then we will restrict the flow of Hashem's Presence in this world. However, John reminds his disciples, "If we confess our sins, he is faithful and just to forgive us our sins and to cleanse us from all unrighteousness" (1 John 1:9). If we do not harbor sin, but continually confess and forsake our shortcomings in the light of the Risen Messiah, we have an enormous potential to be a gateway to heaven that will flood the earth with the Divine Presence of our Creator.

Parashat Kedoshim
LEVITICUS 19:1-20:27

Limiting What Is Permitted

This week's Torah reading covers a lot of territory in a short amount of space. Some of the issues addressed in this portion are honoring one's parents, honoring the Sabbath, how to treat the poor, a detailed explanation of how to love one's neighbor, and a miscellaneous list of other commandments ranging from agricultural laws to prohibitions against sorcery and child sacrifice. Our portion begins, however, with God's instruction that the Children of Israel are to be holy:

> And the LORD spoke to Moses, saying, "Speak to all the congregation of the people of Israel and say to them, You shall be holy, for I the Lord your God am holy." (Lev. 19:1–2)

The name of the portion comes from the instruction, "You shall be holy (*kedoshim*)." The word kedoshim means "holy" (plural). But what does it mean to be holy? A lot of things should be taken into account when we define what it means to be holy, but the primary aspect of holiness is defined through restrictions. This is why God gave the Children of Israel so many "thou shalt not" commandments. He set them apart from the pagan nations around them through restrictions in their conduct, showing that they were to be a holy people.

One way to understand what it means to be holy is to understand what it means to be "unholy." When many people think of something "unholy," they think of something wicked or evil. But that's not what it means. It simply means to be common or, to use King James terminology, "profane." So, if a person is unholy, it just means they are common and like anyone else. To be holy means that we are different from those around us. And one way we can be different, or holy, is to restrict or limit ourselves in the things that the Torah prohibits. But this is obvious. Anyone who studies the Scriptures can pick up on the fact that we are not supposed to engage in commerce on the Sabbath, speak ill of our brother, defraud our neighbor, etc. What is more of a challenge is limiting what is permissible. Our rabbis have taught, "What the Torah forbids is not permitted, but the permitted is not always necessary."

Do we really need that third helping of dessert? Do we really need over 300 channels on our televisions? Do we really need the dozens of video games covering our shelves? Do we really need that ... ? You fill in the blank. By not limiting ourselves in things that are permissible according to the strict reading of the Torah, we can often find ourselves in a position described by Nachmanides as "disgusting with the permission of the Torah." Even though we may be living strictly according to the "letter of the Law," we could easily find ourselves in a position where the beauty and the wisdom of the Torah begins to lose its luster because our eyes are clouded with the world.

Yeshua warns us against such things when he gives his series of "You have heard it said ... but I say to you" in his famous Sermon on the Mount. In many of these he places a fence around the Torah and reminds us that even though the Torah gives us the right to do such-and-such, it's not always in our best interest to do so, especially when it negatively affects a brother. As Paul reminded the believers at Corinth, *"All things are lawful for me," but not all things are helpful. "All things are lawful for me," but I will not be dominated by anything* (1 Corinthians 6:12). The next time you pass on that extra helping of dessert, or refuse to make a brother pay for damages he is responsible for, remember that you have just taken a step toward holiness and becoming a part of a holy people.

Parashat Emor
LEVITICUS 21:1-24:23

Distinct And Set Apart

Parashat Emor begins where last week's parashah (Kedoshim) left off in its description of holiness and how Israel is to be a set-apart and distinct people. Emor continues this theme of distinction by describing how the *kohanim* (priests) had various restrictions and parameters that were even greater than the Children of Israel in general had. For instance, while it was common for an Israelite to become unclean—keep in mind that being unclean in most cases had nothing to do with sin—a kohen was not permitted to become unclean through being in the presence of a corpse in most instances. The *Kohen Gadol* (the high priest) was restricted even further than his priestly brethren to show his distinct position of service among them. Whereas the Children of Israel were to be distinct among the peoples of the earth, the kohanim were to be distinct among the Children of Israel, and the Kohen Gadol was to be distinct among the kohanim.

Another way this parashah enjoins Israel to be distinct is in their demarcation of time. Chapter 23 spells out the calendar that the people of God are to live by. It begins with God's instruction to His people:

Parashat Emor

> These are the appointed feasts of the LORD that you shall proclaim as holy convocations; they are my appointed feasts. (Leviticus 23:2)

How does a calendar point to holiness? We have to remember that although our English translations designate these times as "appointed feasts," this is not how it reads in the original Hebrew. It says they are *mo'adei Hashem*, or the "appointed times of the LORD." What is an appointed time? It's a time that is set aside to meet with the God of Abraham, Isaac, and Jacob. It's a time He has chosen to meet with His people, and therefore we should make those times a priority. After all, He calls them "my appointed times." If they are important to Him, they should be equally important to His people.

The first holy day it sets apart is the weekly Sabbath:

> Six days shall work be done, but on the seventh day is a Sabbath of solemn rest, a holy convocation. You shall do no work. It is a Sabbath to the LORD in all your dwelling places." (Leviticus 23:2)

From there it lists the other festivals and the details of their observance: *Pesach/Chag HaMatzot* (Passover/Unleavened Bread), *Shavuot* (Pentecost), *Rosh Hashanah* (Trumpets), *Yom Kippur* (Day of Atonement), *Sukkot* (Tabernacles/Booths). Each of these times is described with details on how to make them distinct and set-apart from the other days of the year. They are to be special times where we come into the presence of the King of the Universe to worship Him and receive revelation from Him.

Like Parashat Kedoshim, Parashat Emor emphasizes the importance of distinction of the People of God from those of the nations.

It is our job to be different from the world in what we do, what we wear, what we eat, how we speak, and even what we do on certain days to make them distinct from all others. We are to be a holy people through the keeping of His commandments, as He reminds us in this parashah:

> So you shall keep my commandments and do them: I am the LORD. And you shall not profane my holy name, that I may be sanctified among the people of Israel. I am the LORD who sanctifies you, who brought you out of the land of Egypt to be your God: I am the LORD. (Leviticus 22:31–33)

Don't be afraid to stand out and be different. Be distinct and set-apart for the purposes of the Father in this world.

Parashat Behar

LEVITICUS 25:1-26:2

Points Of Divine Connection

Parashat Behar begins, "The LORD spoke to Moses on Mount Sinai, saying." We get the name of the parashah from this opening line. The word *behar* means "on the mountain." But why do we need to know this information? Didn't all of the commandments and instructions given by Moses originate at Sinai when he was given the Torah in its entirety? Why hasn't the Torah reiterated this fact prior to our current reading? Why do we need to be reminded of this obvious fact?

Maybe it's because of the commandments that follow. What follows this statement is a series of commandments that don't seem rational. For instance, the first commandment is the mitzvah of the *shemitah* (sabbatical) year. Every seventh year, farmers in the land of Israel are to leave their ground fallow: no planting, no tilling, no watering, no harvesting, etc. It must remain completely uncultivated. Not only that, but whatever crops are produced are considered communal property. Any person or any beast may eat freely from it.

The second set of commands revolves around the *Yovel* (Jubilee). The Yovel is the fiftieth year, after seven shemitah cycles. The entire year is to be consecrated and dedicated to the return of property to its original owner. In addition, like during the shemitah, Israel is not to cultivate the land; neither planting nor harvesting.

Next, we have various laws pertaining to the sale of property in relationship to the Yovel, including a series of laws for slaves. And last we have several regulations outlining the procedures for redeeming a poor person who has been sold into slavery.

What is the connection between all of these laws and the reminder we had at the very beginning that these laws were given to Moses on Mt. Sinai? The Torah interjects the fact that Moses received these commandments from Sinai to remind us that Hashem's wisdom is far superior to our own, and that human logic will not always lead us to godliness. Man's wisdom is to work for six days and then take a day off to rest so that he can increase his productivity. Hashem's wisdom is that for six days man should work toward the goal of entering into His presence on the seventh day—a time of holy rest, cessation from our own efforts, worship, prayer, Torah study, and fellowship with the Divine. Man's wisdom is that we should "eat, drink, and be merry, for tomorrow we die." In other words, we should live to indulge ourselves in the pleasures of this world. Hashem's wisdom is that we should eat, drink, and enjoy the delicacies He has provided for us in this world with the single goal of divine worship. We fuel our bodies so that they might better serve our Creator.

These are but a few examples. The point is that when our parashah connects these commandments back to Sinai, we are reminded that everything we do should be connected to the Divine. We should not live lives driven by our animal appetites, but instead by our desire to please our Creator. We should take every opportunity to enjoy His blessings in this world while keeping our focus on Him. Everything we do in life should point us back to Sinai, Yeshua, and our redemption.

Parashat Bechukotai

LEVITICUS 26:3-27:34

The Righteous Delusion

As the final reading and concluding note to the book of Vayikra (Leviticus), Parashat Bechukotai (which means, "in my decrees") makes a final appeal to the Children of Israel by listing out a series of blessings and curses related to whether or not they would be faithful to the terms of the covenant made with them at Sinai. Blessings for obedience and curses for disobedience. One unique component about this portion is its use of the Hebrew word *keiri* (קרי). The word is used only seven times in the entire Bible, all of which in our current Torah portion. Here is its first appearance:

> Then if you walk contrary (*keiri*) to me and will not listen to me, I will continue striking you, sevenfold for your sins. (Leviticus 26:21)

In each of these instances it is used in relationship to living a life not in accordance to the Torah. The way it's typically translated is related to being contrary, hostile, or stubborn. Since the Torah seems to be speaking of a rebellious person, it seems obvious that our word in question should be translated along these lines. However, Rashi, the medieval Jewish scholar and commentator, suggests

Parashat Bechukotai

something entirely different. According to Rashi and his knowledge of Hebrew, keiri has the connotation of casualness or passiveness. This makes for a very different understanding of these passages.

Rashi helps us understand what this means by saying that just as some things appear to happen "by chance," so too will our Torah observance become. In other words, we will behave casually toward the commandments and their performance, and therefore Hashem will act casually toward us.

We are living in the days of keiri, casualness toward Hashem's Torah. Our generation has brought God down to our level. He is no longer holy and revered. We know His requirements, but we are casual in living a spiritually disciplined life. Although we may know the Torah, living out its principles is seldom on our radar. James, the brother of the Master, reminds us of the danger of this:

> But be doers of the word, and not hearers only, deceiving yourselves. (James 1:22)

R. Chiyya taught his disciples something similar. He said, "He who learns [Torah] with no intention of practicing had been better unborn" (Leviticus Rabbah 35:7). The *Yetzer Hara* (the evil inclination) is clever. It does its best to makes us think that we are acting righteously even when we are apathetic about living according the Scriptures. It creates a delusion that is nearly impossible to break through. How can we ever hope to escape its influence? The Midrash tells us that the Torah itself is a protection against the Yetzer Hara. It says that the Torah was given for the purpose of refining man and learning to overcome the negative influence of the Yetzer Hara (Gen. Rabbah 44:1). R. Acha gives us a key to how this works:

> He who learns with the intention of practicing will be privileged to receive the Holy Spirit. As it is written, So that you may be careful to do according to all that is written in it. For then you will make your way prosperous, and then you will have good success. [Joshua 1:8] (Leviticus Rabbah 35:7)

Maybe we've been learning for the wrong reasons. Are we studying Torah for intellectual stimulation or simply to fit into the classification of being "Messianic"? Or are we studying for application? If we're not studying for the sake of application, then we are not fertile ground for the Holy Spirit to work within us. We are simply prolonging the exile, delaying the rebuilding of the Holy Temple and denying the establishment of the Messianic Kingdom on earth. When we study the Torah portions, let's look for application so that the Holy Spirit will be able to use us to change the world through changing ourselves first.

***Chazak! Chazak! V'nitchazeik! Be strong!* Be strong! And may we be strengthened!**

Parashat Bamidbar

NUMBERS 1:1–4:20

The Big Picture

A distinct way of reading the Scriptures is evident when we peel back the layers of religious and cultural sediment that have accumulated in our minds. One of the ways to do this is by returning to the original language of the Torah. A prime example of this is found in the book of Numbers. In Christian tradition, the book of Numbers is so named because of the first four chapters, which seem to be written by the Israelite Census Bureau. It appears to be entirely preoccupied by the numbers of the various tribes and subgroups within the Children of Israel. From the opening lines of, "Take a census of all of the congregation of the people of Israel by clans" (1:2) until the end of chapter four, it appears that the Torah has little to offer us other than its obsession with the number of people in the various camps within Israel. But are numbers the only thing the Torah is trying to communicate to us in this parashah?

How we read the Torah depends on our perspective. One person's way of reading a passage may differ vastly from another's. For the casual reader, making it through the first four chapters of the book of Bamidbar is nothing less than an endurance test. If we are oblivious to the big picture, our current reading can seem like a waste of time. However, if we can zoom out and see the bigger picture that the Torah is trying to paint for us, then everything begins to come into focus. Let's briefly zoom out to take a look at one perspective of this.

The name of our parashah is Bamidbar, which is also the Hebrew name of the book of Numbers. But interestingly, the word *bamidbar* doesn't mean "numbers." *Bamidbar* means "in the wilderness," from the word *midbar*, meaning "wilderness." It is taken from the first verse in our reading, "The LORD spoke to Moses *in the wilderness* [*bamidbar*] of Sinai." From the onset of this new book of the Torah, we are given a reminder of the context of what we are about to read. The Children of Israel are no longer slaves in the land of Egypt, nor have they reached the Land of Promise. They are still in the wilderness on their way to Canaan—the land that they will one day call home. Although they are not yet in a time of war, the LORD is having them take a census in preparation for the many battles that lie ahead of them. Entering into the land will not be a waltz in the park; it will require a huge effort on their part. Now is their time of preparation. Now is their time for self-assessment. Now is their time to fine-tune their listening skills so that they can hear their Commander-in-Chief.

Sometimes we feel we are lost in the wilderness. Sometimes we can't see the forest because of the trees. Sometimes the big picture gets lost in the details of everyday life. But if we realize that our Creator has an ultimate game plan, and that our lives are a thread in the tapestry of the Kingdom, we might just be able to zoom out and see the beauty of what He is creating. Just as a tapestry is made up of thousands (if not millions) of individual threads, so too is the tapestry of the Kingdom made up of billions of individuals working toward the purpose of our Creator. It's easy to get frustrated with thread number 3,986,105 and lose sight of the ornate beauty on the other side of the cloth. Are we looking at our lives as merely Numbers in a list or as a Midbar of preparation for our task that is in front of us? Parashat Bamidbar may help us to shift our perspective toward the proper direction if we take it to heart.

Parashat Nasso

NUMBERS 4:21-7:89

Shalom Bayit

Babies. Isn't that what naturally comes to your mind after reading this week's Torah portion? Confused? Let me explain.

This week's reading contains an unusual ritual, the testing of the *sotah* (the wayward wife). This is a strange and even fantastical ritual, quite foreign to the modern mind. To the modern ear it appears to be more akin to alchemy than biblical instruction. It goes like this.

If a woman was suspected of adultery and had been warned in regard to certain actions that could lead to inappropriate behavior, she would be brought to the *kohen* (priest) in the Tabernacle to undergo this unusual interrogation. It begins with her bringing "a grain offering of jealousy, a grain offering of remembrance, bringing iniquity to remembrance" (5:15). The kohen then takes a clay pot filled with sacred water from the bronze laver of the Tabernacle and adds to it some of the dust from the floor of the Tabernacle. He then uncovers her head and places her grain offering into her hands. He then makes her swear an oath. The oath attests to either her innocence or her guilt. If she is innocent, then the waters of cursing will have no effect. If she is guilty, however, then an awful curse will come upon her that will make her "womb swell and [her] thigh fall away" (5:22). After this, the kohen writes the entire curse upon a scroll. He then scrapes off the text—which contains the Divine Name of God—into the water mixture. After this, the woman drinks the mixture of water, dust, and ink and waits to see if her innards will rot.

Does this not seem a bit insane? Why would the Creator of the universe prescribe such a strange ritual filled with such mystical components to be a test against adultery? Why do we need this exotic ritual? The fact of the matter is that human nature has a tendency to incline itself toward doubt and suspicion. A suspicious and jealous husband will never have peace of mind outside of the miraculous. Nothing will ease his mind in regard to the innocence of his wife other than a confirmation from the God of the Universe himself. Therefore, God created this elaborate procedure by which a woman could be either convicted or acquitted in a case where there was just enough evidence to suspect her impropriety, but not enough evidence to convict her by the traditional means. This "trial" would settle the case once and for all. There would be no human witnesses and no jury, but there would also be no doubt. If she suffered an excruciating death, her guilt would be evident. However, if she lived through the process, not only would she be completely released from any suspicion, but she would be rewarded for her endurance. And her reward would be one of the best gifts of all: babies. Yes, her womb would be opened and she would begin bearing children (5:28).

So, what is the point of this mysterious instruction? The ultimate end-game for the test of the sotah is not necessarily the death of an adulteress, but the restoration of a home. Our sages call this ultimate goal *shalom bayit*, or marital harmony (literally a "peaceful home"). Because a healthy marriage is so important, the God of the universe created this elaborate test by which a man and woman could be rejoined as one unit. It is so important to Him that He is willing that His name be erased and mixed with the dust of the earth in order that husband and wife would be reunited. How important is shalom bayit to you?

Parashat Beha'alotcha

NUMBERS 8:1-12:16

To Kindle A Soul

As you have probably noticed, there is almost always something fascinating to discuss at the beginning of the weekly Torah portions. This week is no exception. Parashat Beha'alotcha begins with the instructions on how Aaron, the *Kohen Gadol* (high priest), should kindle the menorah for the Tabernacle:

> Now the LORD spoke to Moses, saying, "Speak to Aaron and say to him, When you set up [baha'alotcha] the lamps, the seven lamps shall give light in front of the lampstand." (Numbers 8:1–2)

The word *baha'alotcha* means, "to cause to go up." Rashi, the medieval Torah commentator, describes this procedure by saying that Aaron was to hold the fire to the wick of the menorah "until the flame rises on its own accord." What does this mean? I'm sure we've all done it. We have lit a match and then held it to a candle until we think the candle is lit. But when we pull the match away and extinguish it, the wick immediately dims and is reduced to a smolder without any sign of a flame. We have wasted not only a match, but also our time. Now we have to find another match and begin the process all over again. Doing it properly, therefore, is to our advantage.

Chasidic Judaism relates Rashi's comment about the kindling of the menorah to discipleship. This concept is connected with Proverbs 20:27, which says that "the soul of man is the candle of God." In other words, the soul of man must be set aflame with the love of God and love of the commandments. Aaron is seen as the model for this. Jewish sources remember Aaron for his ability to endear his fellow man to the Torah. The great sage, Hillel, reminds us that we are to imitate Aaron in this way:

> Be of the disciples of Aaron, loving peace and pursuing peace, loving your fellow creatures and bringing them close to the Torah. (m.Avot 1:12)

Aaron's job was to kindle a flame not only in the menorah, but also in his fellow man. As disciples of Yeshua, we often think it is our job to evangelize others the same way we light candles. We introduce them to the fire within us until we see a spark, and then we move on to the next "candle" before the wick within them is able to produce a flame of its own accord. Therefore, we often end up having to "light" the same people over and over. This is the difference between discipleship and evangelism. Evangelism considers a candle lit if it sparks. Discipleship holds the fire to the candle "until the flame rises on its own accord." If the soul of man is indeed the candle of God, then we need to make sure we hold our flame to it until it is able to be self-sustaining.

How do we do this? Through investing into people's lives. Going door to door or passing out tracts may produce a spark, but rarely does it produce a self-sustaining flame. We must take people under our wings and show them the joy and the beauty of living a godly life. We must also pour into them both the love of God and instruction for righteous living. This takes self-sacrifice, intentional instruction, and a genuine love for others. Only then will the soul of man ignite on its own accord and rise to praise its Creator. Only then will we have helped to create a holy light that does not smolder or grow dim.

Parashat Shelach

NUMBERS 13:1-15:41

The Eyes Of The Heart

This week's Torah reading begins by recounting the spies being sent into the land of Canaan on behalf of the Children of Israel. Joshua, Caleb, and ten other qualified leaders were chosen from each of the twelve tribes and sent into the land of Canaan ahead of the Children of Israel in order to scout out the land and report back their findings, as it says in Numbers 13:2, "Send men to spy out the land of Canaan." As we know, ten of these twelve men came back with an evil report that slandered the land God had promised to them. That evil report delayed their entrance into the Land of Promise by forty long years.

At the end of the portion, we read about how the Children of Israel are to make *tzitzit*—ritual fringes/tassels—on the corners of their garments. Even to this day, religious Jewish men wear a special garment with these tassels attached to it as a normal part of their daily attire. The commandment is as follows:

> Speak to the people of Israel, and tell them to make tassels [*tzitzit*] on the corners of their garments throughout their generations, and to put a cord of blue on the tassel of each corner. And it shall be a tassel for you to look at and

remember all the commandments of the LORD, to do them,
not to follow after your own heart and your own eyes,
which you are inclined to whore after. (Numbers 15:38–39)

How is the beginning of the portion—the evil report of the spies—connected to this seemingly unrelated topic of wearing tassels? In Hebrew, the word used for "spy" is a form of the word *tur* (תור - pronounced "toor"). When we read about the tzitzit, this same word is included in the instructions warning about pursuing after the lusts of our hearts, but we smooth it out in our English translations. The passage literally says that the tzitzit are to be a reminder to not "spy (*tur*) after your own heart and your own eyes." What does this mean? Rashi, in his commentary on this portion, connects these two passages and explains that the eyes and the heart are types of "spies" that search out sins for the body. The eyes see and the heart desires, but the body commits the sin. This kind of language is reminiscent of a teaching by James, the brother of our Master:

> But each person is tempted when he is lured and enticed
> by his own desire. Then desire when it has conceived gives
> birth to sin, and sin when it is fully grown brings forth
> death. (James 1:14–15)

Remember the children's song that says, "Be careful little eyes what you see"? It's true. Our eyes are the gateways to our souls. The temptation for Eve was that she saw that the fruit of the Tree of the Knowledge of Good and Evil was "a delight to the eyes" (Genesis 3:6). The lust of the eyes and the desire of the heart left unchecked will lead us down paths of destruction. The tzitzit are a reminder to guard these gateways and follow the commandments of God. But the tzitzit are not just a reminder to keep the commandments. In a way, they are also a constant reminder to not repeat the same mistake as the spies. Whenever we allow our eyes and our hearts to dictate reality, rather than what God has spoken, we fall prey to the same trap as the ten spies who brought back the evil report. Our reality should be shaped by the Word of God, rather than our own imaginations. The tzitzit are a constant reminder of this.

Parashat Korach

NUMBERS 16:1-18:32

The Test Of Humility

If you've read this week's Torah portion, you already know that the story of Korah is a sad one. But we can learn many important lessons from it. The primary and most obvious lesson we can learn from Korah's mistake is in regard to humility. However, a deeper understanding reveals that his lack of humility stemmed from his disregard for *mishchah*, distinction. Let's explore this further.

Korah was a Levite of the Kohathite family, a cousin of Moses and Aaron. He wasn't just the average Israelite. He had special privileges that the average Israelite did not. Being a Kohathite, he was also responsible for transporting the most holy items in the Tabernacle: the Ark of the Covenant, the table of the showbread, the golden menorah, etc. And as a Levite, he was also supported by the tithe of his Israelite brothers. He was not content, however, to enjoy the privileges of a Levite; he wanted the privileges of the priesthood also. He did not like the distinction between the priests and the Levites. Since the priesthood is determined by birth, Korah felt this was unfair, and his indignation ultimately led him to destruction. He failed the test of humility because he failed to recognize the distinct calling of Aaron's sons. His name will be forever remembered and associated with arrogance, pride, and jealousy.

Parashat Korach

We read about another person in the Scriptures, however, who passed a similar test with flying colors. Once Yeshua was approached by a Gentile woman who begged him to heal her daughter. (See Matthew 15:21-28.) Yeshua's response was shocking. He refused ... and simply because she was a Gentile. He responded, "I was sent only to the lost sheep of the house of Israel. It is not right to take the children's bread and throw it to the dogs." A dog? Really? Is that what she was? Now imagine Korah asking Moses, "Can I please offer the incense, or light the menorah ... just once! Please?" Then imagine Moses responding, "Those things are for the priesthood, Korah! Not for a dog like you!" How do you think he would have responded? This Gentile woman's response was far superior to anything that Korah would have come up with. She replied, "Yes, Lord, yet even the dogs eat the crumbs that fall from their masters' table." She recognized what Yeshua was saying and used it to her advantage. Rather than throwing a fit for being rated a second-class citizen, she recognized the fact that she was not Jewish and was not necessarily entitled to his attention. She then persisted with humility to make her petition and was rewarded for it.

Paul reminds us that we all play a part in God's purposes, whether Jew or Gentile, Levite or priest, apostles, prophets, or teachers:

> The eye cannot say to the hand, "I have no need of you," nor again the head to the feet, "I have no need of you." On the contrary, the parts of the body that seem to be weaker are indispensable, and on those parts of the body that we think less honorable we bestow the greater honor, and our unpresentable parts are treated with greater modesty, which our more presentable parts do not require. But God has so composed the body, giving greater honor to the part that

lacked it, that there may be no division in the body, but that the members may have the same care for one another. (1 Corinthians 12:21–25)

We are all members of one body. When we are not happy with the fact that God has made us all different with different responsibilities, then we will never truly be content with who we are and we will not fulfill the calling He has designed specifically for us. We can choose to be like Korah and reject those differences, or we can be like the Gentile woman who recognized them and used them to her advantage. The choice is ours.

Parashat Chukat

NUMBERS 19:1-22:1

Divine Reversals

This week's Torah portion contains one of the least understood passages in all of the Scriptures. In the beginning of our portion, we have the instructions for the *parah adumah*—the red heifer—whose ashes are mixed with water to create the singular source of ritual purity for specific conditions described within the Torah. For example, only by water mixed with the ashes of the red heifer could a corpse contamination be negated.

One of the mysteries about the red heifer is how purification through its ashes works. The cow is burnt completely along with cedar wood, hyssop, and crimson wool. Then the ashes are gathered up and a small amount is mixed with a large volume of water. Now, by sprinkling this mixture on someone who is considered to have contracted the highest level of ritual impurity, it somehow has the power to transform the status of that person. How does it work? No one knows. That is why this ritual is called a *chok*, a decree or ordinance. It is a command that seems to make no sense to our human minds.

More puzzling, however, is the question of how coming into contact with these ashes makes a ritually pure person become impure. Everyone who comes in contact with the ashes—the priest who oversees the burning, the one who burned the animal, and the

Parashat Chukat

one who collects the ashes—becomes impure. This defies human reasoning. And yet the solution to the problem of one who has become defiled through the ashes of the red heifer is an immersion in water. Water, therefore, is a common denominator in transmitting ritual purity. However, we have an example of when water can actually be a source of ritual impurity:

> A spring or a cistern holding water shall be clean, but whoever touches a carcass in them shall be unclean. And if any part of their carcass falls upon any seed grain that is to be sown, it is clean, but if water is put on the seed and any part of their carcass falls on it, it is unclean to you. (Leviticus 11:36–38)

How do these things work? We may never know. But we see another example of this seemingly counterintuitive series of reversals in the Apostolic Scriptures. Yeshua came to this earth in order to bring redemption to all of humanity. However, many among the spiritual leaders of Israel rejected him. How can this be? Were they hard-hearted, blind, or uneducated in the Scriptures? Why was Yeshua a stumbling block for some, but not for others? Let's ask this question: Why do some medicines make one person well and another sick? It is the same medicine. When it is given to one who is ill, it can aid him in his recovery. But when given to a person who is well, it has the potential to cause serious problems.

Yeshua functioned like the red heifer. He himself said that he did not come for those who were well, but for those who were sick and needing a physician (Mark 2:17). His mission was not to the righteous, but to the sinner. Thus, contact with the living Messiah was a source of cleansing for the sinner, but it was also a source of contamination for the righteous. Just as we cannot explain the mechanics of how the ashes of the red heifer work, neither can we satisfactorily explain how contact with Yeshua transforms a sinner or a saint. We do know, however, that once we have an encounter with him, we will never be the same.

Parashat Balak

NUMBERS 22:2-25:9

Looking For Loopholes

The portion of Balak is filled with supernatural interactions between God and a Gentile prophet by the name of Balaam. From our portion, Balaam appears to have been renowned for his spiritual acumen, and seems to have a close relationship with the God of Abraham, Isaac, and Jacob. Yet in the end we find that he is dead set on destroying the Children of Israel. How did this come about? Let's take a brief look at Balaam's mistake.

When Balak's men came to Balaam and asked him to curse Israel, he realized that his services would fetch a large sum of money. He had only one problem. He couldn't speak anything more than what God would allow him:

> "Though Balak were to give me his house full of silver and gold, I could not go beyond the command of the LORD my God to do less or more." (Numbers 22:18)

How would he be able to bring a curse upon Israel? Our sages tell us, however, that this was a mixture of truth and a lie. Truth, in that Balaam was indeed limited by what God allowed him to speak. But also a lie, in that his answer masked the greed hidden in

Parashat Balak

Balaam's heart. Balaam's Achilles' heel was his evil eye—greed—as it is said:

> The evil eye, the evil desire and hatred of his fellow creatures put a man out of the world. (Avot 2:16)

How do we know this? Not only do Rashi and other ancient commentators mention this, but we also have the Apostolic testimony:

> They have followed the way of Balaam, the son of Beor, who loved gain from wrongdoing. (2 Peter 2:15)

> Woe to them! For they walked in the way of Cain and abandoned themselves for the sake of gain to Balaam's error and perished in Korah's rebellion. (Jude 11)

But if Balaam could speak only what God told him to, how did he ever hope to accomplish his wicked task of cursing Israel? When he asked permission initially, he received an explicit "No!" If that was the case, why did he ask again? Because when God appeared to Balaam during the night and asked, "Who are these men with you?" Balaam began to think that God was not omniscient like he had previously believed. Therefore, if he could just get God's permission to go with the men, he might be able to accomplish his mission before he was found out. So he asked permission again. This time, God allowed him to go with Balak's men. Did God change his mind? Why did He say no the first time and yes the second time?

When Balaam initially asked permission to go with Balak's men, God told him to not go with them (*imahem* in Hebrew). But when God ended up giving Balaam permission, He used a different Hebrew word than before. He said that Balaam may go with them, *itam*. Our sages explain that the difference between these words is that the first implies being one in purpose, while the second implies merely physically accompanying someone. Balaam was to go with them, but he was not supposed to join in their wicked schemes. Evidently, Balaam didn't pay attention to the wording and assumed he had permission from the Almighty to be in collusion with Moab.

Have we ever asked God for permission about something and were given a definite "no," but then preceded to ask again? Have we ever been guilty of looking for loopholes in the Scriptures? Balaam's mistake was to think that God's "no" wasn't His final answer. When God says something, it's His final word. As Balaam himself ended up proclaiming, "God is not man, that he should lie, or a son of man, that he should change his mind" (Numbers 23:19). If God doesn't change His mind, why would we pretend that He does? Therefore, rather than acting like a child throwing a tantrum when God says no, we should realize that His wisdom is above ours, His answer is always best, and His ways are always good. To the only wise God be glory forevermore through Messiah Yeshua! Amen (Romans 16:27).

Parashat Pinchas

NUMBERS 25:10-30:1[29:40]

The Bulls Of Our Lips

This week's portion covers a variety of topics: the reward of Pinchas, a new census of the Israelites, a case of inheritance in regard to the daughters of Zelophehad, the succession of Joshua, and then in the next two chapters is a series of laws regulating the types of offerings that were to be brought to the Holy Temple for various occasions. This last section is what I would like to draw our attention to.

It begins by describing the *tamid* (continual) offerings—two lambs every morning and late afternoon—that were offered up as whole burnt offerings in the Holy Temple every single day. God considered these daily offerings very special. He lets us know that He desires them at specific times of the day, instructing the Children of Israel about them, saying, "You shall be careful to offer to me at its appointed time" (28:2). He said they are "my offering, my food for my food offerings, my pleasing aroma." He considered them personal gifts from the Children of Israel that He received twice daily, three hundred and sixty-five days a year.

Today, however, the Holy Temple does not stand in Jerusalem. Only its ruins remain. These offerings that are dear to the LORD can no longer be offered. So what can we do to ensure we are bringing to

Parashat Pinchas

God what He has asked each day? With the destruction of the first Temple during the Babylon exile, the Jewish people had this same dilemma. How were they supposed to continue giving to God what He required without a Temple? Fortunately, they came up with a solution. Our sages looked into the Scriptures and realized that God had already provided them an answer. Nearly two hundred years before, the prophet Hosea had written these words:

> Take with you words, and turn to the LORD; say unto Him, "Take away all iniquity and receive us graciously, so will we offer the calves of our lips." (Hosea 14:2, KJV)

In other words, in the place where we would normally offer up bulls as whole burnt offerings, God would accept the offerings of our lips as an equivalent substitution. And if God accepted our prayers in place of whole burnt offerings, then prayer would also be the acceptable substitution for the daily offerings until the time when the Holy Temple would be restored. Prayer would now take on as much importance as these daily sacrifices that could not be offered. Therefore, just as the lambs were offered morning and evening each day, our prayers are offered at the time that these lambs would have been slaughtered as a continuous offering before the LORD.

As we can see, our daily prayers are intimately connected with the daily sacrificial services that took place in the Holy Temple, and are a crucial component of every day. Therefore, we pray specific prayers at these specific times every day. Joining together with the community of Israel in one voice during these favorable times should be the bare minimum of our divine "service of the heart." Together, we can be participants to ensure that God is receiving the very thing He asked of us. These daily prayers connect us back to ancient past, empower our present life, and help us to anticipate an epic future event when the Kingdom is restored to Israel and Messiah Yeshua sits upon his throne, reigning from Jerusalem. Messianic Jewish pioneer Paul Philip Levertoff said, "If only all of Israel could pray correctly, then the Messiah would already be here, revealed in his glory." May we be Kingdom participants in this important daily endeavor, and may we merit to see the return of our King soon and in our day.

Parashat Mattot

NUMBERS 30:2[1]-32:42

A Lesson of Priorities

When we read the first verse of Numbers 32, it seems pretty normal in English. It tells us how the lush pasturelands of Jazer and Gilead were suitable for the large number of cattle owned by the tribes of Reuben and Gad:

> Now the people of Reuben and the people of Gad had a very great number of livestock. And they saw the land of Jazer and the land of Gilead, and behold, the place was a place for livestock. (Numbers 32:1)

If we look at the Hebrew behind this verse, however, we will find a much more dynamic description of what is taking place. Once we discover this, we will learn a valuable lesson in priorities.

In Hebrew, this verse should initially get our attention because it both begins and ends with the same word: *mikneh*, or "cattle/livestock." It also contains word repetitions and several emphasis words, such as *rav* (great), *atzum* (vast/numerous), and *meod* (exceedingly/much). If we were to translate this verse into English to retain the emphases of the Hebrew, it might sound something like this:

Parashat Mattot

> Cattle—abundant—had the children of Reuben and the children of Gad—great and vast amounts— and behold, they saw that the land of Jazer and the land of Gilead—that place—was a place for cattle.

The Torah has a wealth of knowledge to offer on the mere surface level. Often, however, it desires to teach us a deeper lesson that we are not able to perceive through our translations without assistance. Sometimes a lesson is waiting to be learned just below the surface of the text if we will take the time to unearth it. After all, it is the glory of God to conceal a matter, but the glory of kings to search it out (Proverbs 25:2).

When we dig into this passage, we should ask ourselves, "Who has who? Do Reuben and Gad have the cattle? Or do the cattle have Reuben and Gad?" It's apparent that the Torah is about to teach us a lesson of priorities.

The tribes of Reuben and Gad not only ask permission to stay behind while the other tribes go and fight to settle the land of Canaan, but they also have their priorities all mixed up. They tell Moses, "the land ... is a land for livestock, and your servants have livestock" (Numbers 32:4). When Moses scolds them, they say they will "build sheepfolds [for their] livestock, and cities for [their] little ones" (v. 16) before they go and fight for the Land of Promise. Taking care of their children almost seems to be an afterthought in relationship to their plans for their livestock. Again, Moses has to correct them and straighten out their priorities by reversing the order and telling them, "Build cities for your little ones and folds for your sheep" (v. 24).

Reuben and Gad had their priorities in their livestock. Moses wanted their priorities to be in their families. But the Torah had already foreshadowed this problem by telling us that the tribes of Reuben and Gad had more livestock than they knew what to do with. But did they have the livestock, or did the livestock have them?

Where are our priorities? What do we think about and talk about the most? Do we have our possessions, or do our possessions have us? The answer may be deeper than we think.

Parashat Massei

NUMBERS 33:1-36:13

The Laws of Inheritance

Parashat Massei is the final portion in the book of Bamidbar (Numbers). This portion begins in chapter 33 by recounting the various encampments made by the Children of Israel during their years subsequent to their exodus from Egypt. Chapter 34 defines the borders given to the Children of Israel as their inheritance, and chapter 35 outlines the cities given to the Levites. In the final chapter, Numbers 36, we learn some foundational principles regarding biblical inheritance. But before we get into this account, we need to understand a couple of inheritance issues.

First, although this matter has been under scrutiny in recent years, according to Jewish law, Jewish identity is inherited through the mother. This explains why Paul, who is very outspoken in his epistles against circumcision for Gentiles, has one of his disciples circumcised and another one remain uncircumcised. According to Galatians 2, Titus, who is clearly not Jewish ("he was a Greek," Galatians 2:3), is not obligated to take on circumcision. Since he is Greek and does not have a Jewish mother, he is under no compulsion to be circumcised.

This is not the case, however, with his disciple Timothy. According to the account in Acts 16, Timothy is never referred to as a Greek. He was "the son of a Jewish woman" whose "father was a Greek" (vs. 1–3). This made him *halachically* (legally) Jewish. His father, being a Greek, probably did not want him circumcised as a child and therefore Paul urged Timothy to fulfill his obligation as an adult to take on the sign of the covenant by way of circumcision. Timothy's Jewish identity, inherited through his mother, mandated his need for circumcision.

Second, although Jewish identify is inherited matrilineally, tribal identity is a patrilineal inheritance. For example, John the Immerser's father, Zechariah, was a kohen (priest) in the line of Abijah (Luke 1:5). This makes John a kohen also. Paul, a Benjamite by tribal affiliation, was so because his father was also descended from Benjamin. Understanding these two laws helps explain the problem of intermarriage in Ezra 9–10, and why Ezra had the men of Israel divorce and send away their foreign wives along with their children.

Finally, our current parashah concludes with the incident involving the daughters of Zelophehad. This incident addresses two issues of inheritance: material inheritance of daughters and tribal affiliation of wives. In this unique case, a man named Zelophehad, of the tribe of Manasseh, had five unmarried daughters. However, he died before producing any male offspring. Since he had no male offspring, his inheritance was divided between his daughters. This produced a problem concerning inheritance, and the potential transfer of inheritance through intermarriage. Their kinsmen spoke up:

> If they are married to any of the sons of the other tribes of the people of Israel, then their inheritance will be taken from the inheritance of our fathers and added to the inheritance of the tribe into which they marry. (Numbers 36:3)

Since property inheritance was passed down through the males, it remained within the tribal possession no matter how many times it was inherited. However, problems arose when a daughter inherited. To whom did ownership pass upon her marriage? It is assumed that once a woman was married she took on the tribal identity of her husband. This would cause the property to be taken from the tribal boundaries originally assigned to it.

As one can see, this would quickly become a problem. Rather than having boundaries for the regions of Judah, Dan, Naphtali, etc. the land would be divided up into a patchwork landscape of tribal boundaries that would change from year to year. In order to remedy this potential problem, Hashem told Moses:

> Every daughter who possesses an inheritance in any tribe of the people of Israel shall be wife to one of the clan of the tribe of her father ... So no inheritance shall be transferred from one tribe to another. (Numbers 36:8–9)

The solution was for daughters who had inherited property to marry only within their tribe. If they did not own property, however, they were free to marry into any tribe. Only if they owned property were they bound to this restriction.

Why does any of this matter? Because Israel belongs to God, and He cares for it dearly. Although most Believers are not concerned with the land given to the Children of Israel and its ownership, to Hashem—the God of Abraham, Isaac, and Jacob—it is of great concern:

> The eyes of the LORD your God are always upon it, from the beginning of the year to the end of the year. (Deuteronomy 11:12)

The laws of property inheritance for the Children of Israel within the Promised Land unfortunately are not applicable today. Why? Because Israel is not ruled over by the principles of a Torah-modeled government. One day, however, King Messiah will reign from Jerusalem and the Torah will go forth from Zion and the laws of the Kingdom will be reestablished. May it be soon and in our lifetime, Amen.

***Chazak! Chazak! V'nitchazeik!* Be strong! Be strong! And may we be strengthened!**

Parashat Devarim

DEUTERONOMY 1:1-3:22

Faith and Disbelief

In our Torah portion this week, Moses begins by giving a brief overview of the last forty years of the Children of Israel's journeys in the wilderness. One of the first events he brings to their attention is the evil report about the Land, and how that report put fear into their hearts, keeping them from entering the Land as the LORD intended. He makes a point to remind them that, because of this one event, all of God's plans for them were put on hold and they had been suffering the consequences of this for the last forty years:

> Then I said to you, "Do not be in dread or afraid of them. The LORD your God who goes before you will himself fight for you, just as he did for you in Egypt before your eyes, and in the wilderness, where you have seen how the LORD your God carried you, as a man carries his son, all the way that you went until you came to this place." Yet in spite of this word you did not believe in the LORD your God. (Deuteronomy 1:29-32)

In this rebuke, he says that the Children of Israel "did not believe in the LORD your God" (1:32). What did Moses mean when he said that they did not *believe* in God? Does it mean they didn't believe in His existence? How could they not? They had seen His miracles, His signs, and wonders. They had seen His deliverance firsthand! So what did Moses mean?

If we backtrack a few verses, we will find the real issue at hand. Moses reminds them of how they initially responded when they received the instruction to enter the Land. They said, "Because the LORD hated us he has brought us out of the land of Egypt" (Deuteronomy 1:27). Because He *hated* them? Yes, their disbelief in God wasn't about whether or not they believed in His existence or if He had the ability to do miracles on their behalf. Their disbelief was rooted in their doubt of God's love for them. Sure, He could do incredible things, but why didn't He just remove all of the obstacles and teleport them into the Promised Land? Why did they still have to fight and toil and labor if God really loved them? This was one aspect of their disbelief. Let's look at another.

The Hebrew root behind this word "believe" is *emunah*. It is the same word we translate as "faith." But let's look at its very first use in the Bible to discover something interesting. When Israel was battling against Amalek, the position of Moses' hands was important to their victory:

> Whenever Moses held up his hand, Israel prevailed, and whenever he lowered his hand, Amalek prevailed. But Moses' hands grew weary, so they took a stone and put it under him, and he sat on it, while Aaron and Hur held up his hands, one on one side, and the other on the other side. So his hands were steady until the going down of the sun. And Joshua overwhelmed Amalek and his people with the sword. (Exodus 17:11–13)

When it says Moses' hands were "steady," the original word is *emunah*. In other words, Moses' hands remained faithful and true. They did not waiver. Due to the assistance of Aaron and Hur, Moses' hands remained true the entire day throughout the course of the battle. They could be trusted to not fail.

To have emunah in someone or something is to place a confiding trust in them, so much so that you are devoted to them despite the challenges that may arise along the journey of life. In a relationship, that means both trust and devotion are central. When one of these components is missing, the relationship will crumble. One person may have trust in God, but not faithfulness. Another might have faithfulness, but not trust. Both of these scenarios, however, lack true faith. True, biblical faith is expressed through both trust and faithfulness. When we apply this to our relationship with God, we must ask ourselves if we are expressing both of these qualities. If we are lacking either one, then our faith in Him is lacking also.

Parashat Va'etchanan

DEUTERONOMY 3:23-7:11

Eating Elephants (Kosher Ones, That Is)

Have you ever been overwhelmed at what seemed like an impossible task? We can respond to this in one of two ways. The first is to give up without even trying, because we instantly know that we will not be able to complete the task. The alternative, however, is to get our minds off of the impossibility of the task and onto the responsibility at hand. If we focus on the immediate requirements of the task and work our hardest on what we *can* do, then we might accomplish more than we realize.

Moses was faced with a similar problem in this week's Torah portion. In Deuteronomy 4 we read, "Then Moses set apart three cities in the east beyond the Jordan." But the problem with this verse is that this is not actually what it says in the original Hebrew. If we were to read the actual Hebrew text, we would understand it to say, "Then Moses *will* set apart three cities." This helps us understand why most translations change this to read in the past tense. It doesn't seem to make sense on the surface that Moses will, at some point in the future, separate these cites of refuge. How is Moses going to do this at some future time if he has been barred from entering into the Holy Land? Moses had a problem without a solution in sight. He had been given an impossible task.

Many people look at the task of living out a Torah-centered life in a similar way. We've wrongly been taught for far too long that living out the commandments of Torah is impossible. Therefore, most people shrug it off without much thought. "No one can live it out perfectly," many have said. But are we required to live out the precepts of the Torah flawlessly? Or are we commanded to give our best efforts every day?

A parable: One day a man was walking along the beach early in the morning and noticed hundreds of thousands of precious stones and pearls that had washed up onto the beach during the night. They covered the beach as far as the eye could see. Does he get depressed or give up when he realizes he will never be able to collect every last item that has washed up on the shore? Or does he become elated because he can collect as many as possible with any means he has? This should be our response to the overwhelming number of commandments in the Torah. We should rejoice in the few that we can observe and long for the ones we are currently missing out on. They are the precious "gems" given to us by our Creator and Redeemer. Yes, the task may be impossible to complete, but it is not impossible to embark on. As Rabbi Tarfon would say, "It is not incumbent upon you to finish the task, but neither are you free to absolve yourself from it" (Avot 2:16).

Even though Moses knew he could not enter the Promised Land, and therefore could not personally work to establish these three cities of refuge, he nonetheless took up the task and began working toward their realization. Do we have the ability to bring back Yeshua and initiate the Messianic Era? Maybe not, but we can definitely work toward their realization through faithfully living out the precepts given to us within the Torah and the rest of the Scriptures. Will we be able to live them out perfectly? No. We will just have to work on them a little bit every day until Yeshua's return. As they say: How do you eat an elephant (a kosher one, of course)? One bite at a time.

Parashat Ekev

DEUTERONOMY 7:12-11:25

The Mitzvah of Gratitude

In Judaism, we have the practice of giving thanks after each meal. This is called *Birkat HaMazon*, or Grace After Meals. This practice is derived from the passage in our Torah portion that gives the instruction to thank the LORD after eating:

> And you shall eat and be full, and you shall bless the LORD your God for the good land he has given you. (Deuteronomy 8:10)

But isn't it only natural for a person to give thanks for what they have received? Why do we need a commandment to require this of us? Let's look at an example from the Apostolic Scriptures that will bring us some clarification:

> And as he [Yeshua] entered a village, he was met by ten lepers, who stood at a distance and lifted up their voices and said, "Yeshua, Master, have mercy on us!" When he saw them he said to them, "Go and show yourselves to the priests." And as they went they were cleansed. Then one of them, when he saw that he was healed, turned back, prais-

Parashat Ekev

> ing God with a loud voice; and he fell on his face at Yeshua's feet, giving him thanks. Now he was a Samaritan. Then said Yeshua, "Were not ten cleansed? Where are the nine? Was no one found to return and give praise to God except this foreigner?" And he said to him, "Rise and go your way; your faith has made you well." (Luke 17:12–19)

In this incident, all ten lepers were healed by Yeshua, yet only one returned to thank him. In order to understand why, we need take a peek into a concept in Hebrew. In Hebrew, the expression for gratitude is *hakarat hatov*, which literally means "recognizing the good." Once we understand this concept, we can find traces of this Semitic expression embedded into our Gospel narrative. It says that "when he saw that he was healed," he turned back to praise God and thank Yeshua. Yeshua asked him, "Were not ten cleansed?" Indeed, ten were cleansed, but only one "recognized the good" that was done to him.

What about the other nine? They were like the majority of us. If Yeshua had asked them what they would give to be healed, they would probably have given anything in the world. But once they were healed—once they were satisfied—they quickly forgot their desperate need that existed only moments before. This is why we need a commandment that tells us to be grateful and to express that gratitude once we have satisfied our need. We are a forgetful people, especially when it comes to the blessings poured out on us. Immediately after the commandment is given, the LORD explains why we are instructed to give thanks once we have been satiated:

> Take heed lest you forget the LORD your God, by not keeping his commandments and his ordinances and his statutes,

which I command you this day: lest, when you have eaten and are full ... then your heart be lifted up, and you forget the LORD your God, who brought you out of the land of Egypt, out of the house of bondage (Deuteronomy 8:11–12,14)

Becoming more intentional is a step toward overcoming our human nature of forgetfulness and ungratefulness. Once we begin practicing the mitzvah of gratitude, we will find that we have a more thankful heart. Not only that, but we will be blessed. We will have recognized the good and begun our journey toward a more fulfilling life.

Parashat Re'eh

DEUTERONOMY 11:26-16:17

The Snowball Effect

Have you ever heard of the Snowball Effect? As you know, the Snowball Effect is a process that begins with something that is seemingly insignificant but then builds on itself, becoming exponentially larger over time. It comes from the concept of a snowball rolling down a hill. In theory, it picks up both mass and momentum the longer it rolls. After just a little while it would become quite massive and very difficult to stop. This concept has been applied to many things, but it has spiritual applications as well. In Pirkei Avot, Ben Azzai tells us:

> Run to pursue a minor mitzvah [commandment], and flee from a transgression. For a mitzvah brings another mitzvah, and a transgression brings another transgression. For the reward of a mitzvah is a mitzvah, and the reward of transgression is transgression. (m.Avot 4:2)

This is the principle of the Snowball Effect. If we begin traveling in a certain direction—whether toward or away from spiritual matters—we will create a momentum that will be difficult to stop. If we succeed in surrendering one area of our lives and being obedient to

Parashat Re'eh

one instruction from the Torah, we will naturally be inclined toward the next one. We will find that obedience will have become a little easier. However, the reverse is also true. If we refuse to be obedient to one of the Torah's instructions, then it will be more difficult to obey other instructions. Soon we will find ourselves in a place of utter rebellion, where even the easiest commandments are forsaken. This is the principle behind the introductory words of this week's Torah portion:

> See, I am setting before you today a blessing and a curse: the blessing, if you obey the commandments of the LORD your God, which I command you today, and the curse, if you do not obey the commandments of the LORD your God, but turn aside from the way that I am commanding you today, to go after other gods that you have not known. (Deuteronomy 11:26–28)

The LORD tells us that He gives us two choices: a blessing or a curse. The blessing comes about through obedience and the curse through disobedience. Every day we have the choice to enjoy blessings or curses. Every day we have the choice to either obey or disobey. Each one of these choices will produce its own fruit. Obedience brings a blessing and disobedience brings a curse. Once we make our choice and embark on the journey of obedience or disobedience, we will find that it is easier to continue down that same path than it is to turn around and head in the opposite direction. The Didache, one of the earliest non-canonical teachings of the Apostles, explains the ramifications of this choice:

Parashat Re'eh

> There are two ways, one of life and one of death, and the difference between the two ways is great. (Didache 1:1)

Does anyone ever wake up in the morning and say, "I think I'll do evil today"? Possibly. But by far most of humanity does not. We don't usually set out on the wrong path with intention. However, we might end up on that path if we do not take calculated steps to avoid it. Therefore, if we combine the warning of the Torah with the explanation of Ben Azzai, we will see the ramifications of choosing the proper path:

> See, I am setting before you today a blessing and a curse: the blessing, if you obey the commandments of the LORD your God, which I command you today, and the curse, if you do not obey the commandments of the LORD your God. ... Run to pursue a minor mitzvah, and flee from a transgression. For a mitzvah brings another mitzvah, and a transgression brings another transgression. For the reward of a mitzvah is a mitzvah, and the reward of transgression is transgression.

Let's get that snowball rolling. Let's take intentional steps today to pursue blessings through obedience so that everything we do for the Kingdom will be multiplied exponentially.

Parashat Shoftim

DEUTERONOMY 16:18–21:9

Remembrance and Redemption

As one exits the Yad Vashem Holocaust museum in Jerusalem, the final site is a sign written in Hebrew and in English. It is a profound quote from the Baal Shem Tov, the founder of Chassidic Judaism in the eighteenth century:

> Forgetfulness leads to exile, while remembrance is the secret of redemption.

What does this mean? Let's explore the implications. According to our Torah portion for this week, the king of Israel is commanded to write a copy of the Torah for himself as a reminder of his responsibilities as the leader of a holy nation bound to a covenant relationship with the Creator of the Universe:

> And when he sits on the throne of his kingdom, he shall write for himself in a book a copy of this law, approved by the Levitical priests. And it shall be with him, and he shall read in it all the days of his life, that he may learn to fear the LORD his God by keeping all the words of this law and these statutes, and doing them, that his heart may not be

Parashat Shoftim

> lifted up above his brothers, and that he may not turn aside from the commandment, either to the right hand or to the left. (Deuteronomy 17:18–20)

The king of Israel represents the nation of Israel. Therefore, when the king is diligent to uphold the Torah, he is considered righteous and the nation is blessed. But when the king forgets the precepts of the Torah, he is deemed wicked and the nation is therefore judged and led into exile.

Since the king represents Israel, some of his responsibilities also represent those of individual citizens. Deuteronomy 31:19 says, "Now therefore write this song and teach it to the people of Israel." This is considered to be the very last in the enumeration of the 613 commandments, and is interpreted to mean that every Jewish person is obligated to in some way—often through contributing to the production of a new Torah scroll—write for himself a copy of the Torah. Just as the king is obligated to have his own copy of the Torah to study, so are his citizens.

As citizens of the Kingdom, it would behoove us to possess a copy of the Torah in the form of a Chumash (a book that contains both the Hebrew and English of the Torah along with commentary) and study it daily. Through constant, daily study it will sink into our hearts in order that we "may not turn aside from the commandment, either to the right hand or to the left," but follow the LORD wholeheartedly. If we do this while clinging to our righteous Messiah, we have the potential to become emissaries of the Messianic Era in our present, broken world. Through this process, we can get a glimpse into the hope that the prophet Jeremiah says awaits us:

> Behold, the days are coming, declares the LORD, when I will make a new covenant with the house of Israel and the house of Judah. ... I will put my law within them, and I will write it on their hearts. And I will be their God, and they shall be my people. And no longer shall each one teach his neighbor and each his brother, saying, "Know the LORD," for they shall all know me, from the least of them to the greatest, declares the LORD. (Jeremiah 31:31, 33–34)

Until the time when the Torah is written on our hearts and a man will not have to teach his neighbor, we would do well to study it every day so that we "may not turn aside from the commandment, either to the right hand or to the left." But until then, we must study the Torah diligently every day to discern the "good and perfect will of God" in our lives, and be faithful in all that He has called us to. Indeed, forgetfulness leads to exile, but remembrance is the key to unlocking redemption. Will you help bring *tikkun* (repair) to the world by remembering what others have forgotten?

Parashat Ki Tetze

DEUTERONOMY 21:10-25:19

His Eye Is On The Sparrow

Have you ever wondered what the "least of the commandments" is that Yeshua speaks of in Matthew 5? (See Matthew 5:17-20.) According to our sages, the least commandment is found in this week's Torah portion:

> If you come across a bird's nest in any tree or on the ground, with young ones or eggs and the mother sitting on the young or on the eggs, you shall not take the mother with the young. You shall let the mother go, but the young you may take for yourself, that it may go well with you, and that you may live long. (Deuteronomy 12:6-7)

Sending away the mother bird is considered to be the least or the "lightest" of the commandments. It requires no great effort on the part of the one performing the commandment. It is considered an act of compassion, similar to the commandment in Leviticus that says, "You shall not kill an ox or a sheep and her young in one day" (Leviticus 22:28). Other commandments, however, are more weighty. They require more effort and seem to have more significance than others. For instance, honoring one's father and mother is considered one of the most weighty or important commandments. But the division between light and heavy commandments is somewhat artificial. Yes, the distinction exists, but they are all to be followed equally. Rabbi Judah explains:

> Be as scrupulous about a light commandment as a weighty one, for you do not know the reward allotted for each commandment. (Avot 2:1)

Why does he say this? Because we are told the reward for both a light commandment (the sending away of the mother bird) and a heavy commandment (honoring one's parents) is the same—long life:

> Honor your father and your mother, as the LORD your God commanded you, that your days may be long, and that it may go well with you in the land that the LORD your God is giving you. (Deuteronomy 5:16)

Yeshua agreed with Rabbi Judah that his disciples should observe even the least of the commandments with as much attention as the greatest commandments. He said, "Whoever relaxes one of the least of these commandments and teaches others to do the same will be called least in the kingdom of heaven" (Matthew 5:19). Yeshua would have had in mind commandments such as sending away the mother bird as "the least of these commandments" when he was teaching his disciples. But do we honor his teachings?

Unfortunately, the large majority of Yeshua followers believe that his Father's instructions—"the Law"—have been abolished, despite this being exactly the opposite of what Yeshua said. Yeshua would never tell his disciples that his Father's instructions were outdated, had no more relevance, or should be abandoned. Therefore, neither should we. Our Heavenly Father is still as compassionate today as He was when the book of Deuteronomy and the commandment to send away the mother bird were written. Why would we think otherwise? After all, His eye is still on the sparrow.

# Parashat Ki Tavo

DEUTERONOMY 26:1-29:8[9]

Our Coming In And Our Going Out

When the Torah says things in an unusual way, it's usually to teach us an important lesson. Normally, when we think of a person's comings and goings, it is from the perspective of first leaving a place and then returning to it. The Torah, however, has a different frame of reference:

> Blessed shall you be when you come in, and blessed shall you be when you go out. (Deuteronomy 28:6)

According to the Torah, a person first enters and then departs. Rabbi Yochanan interprets this to mean that our coming in and going out are the points by which we enter and depart from this world:

> "Blessed shalt thou be when thou comest in, and blessed shalt thou be when thou goest out" — that thine exit from the world shall be as thine entry therein: just as thou enterest it without sin, so mayest thou leave it without! (b.Bava Metzia 107a)

The point at which man comes into this world is his birth; his going out is his death. The thing we call life is that short span between these two points. We are merely sojourners during the course of our life here in this world.

Rabbi Yochanan connects these two points of entrance and departure with the common theme of blessing. He says that just as a person enters this world without sin, a person is truly blessed if he is also able to leave this world without sin. But how do we do this? Is it even possible? Evidently, Paul thought it was. His hope was to deliver his disciples into the hands of Yeshua "pure and blameless":

> And it is my prayer that your love may abound more and more, with knowledge and all discernment, so that you may approve what is excellent, and so be pure and blameless for the day of Christ, filled with the fruit of righteousness that comes through Jesus Christ, to the glory and praise of God. (Philippians 1:9–11)

But in order to present ourselves pure and blameless at the end of our days, we must make every moment count of the time allotted to us in this world. We must work to purge ourselves from the control of our flesh and take upon ourselves the yoke of the Kingdom every single day. The good news Yeshua offered was one of repentance in anticipation of the coming Kingdom. He taught us that the rest of our lives did not have to be wasted like our previous days, months, or years. Through sincere repentance we could cleanse our past and alter our future—and not only our future, but the future of others as well.

Yeshua taught several parables connected to the final accounting of the soul. Matthew 25 records Yeshua teaching the Parable of the Ten Virgins and the Parable of the Talents leading up to his teaching about the final judgment. His point in these teachings is for us to be prepared for the day we would be presented back to our Creator.

We are in this world only for a limited time. Rabbi Jacob used to say, "This world is like a hallway to the future world. Prepare yourself in the hallway that you may enter into the banquet hall" (Avot 4:21). We are not promised tomorrow. We must be prepared for our departure. We must make every moment count so that we can depart as blameless as when we entered this world. How will you spend today? Tomorrow? The days following? How will you use the time you have been given today to prepare for your departure tomorrow? Will you invest your time into becoming all that you were created for, or will you squander your time here and be ashamed on the day of reckoning? May your departure from this vestibule be as blessed as your entrance into it.

Parashat Nitzavim
DEUTERONOMY 29:9[10]-30:20

The Hidden And The Revealed

This week's Torah portion is a continuation of Moses' adjuration to the Children of Israel to faithfully obey the instructions the LORD has given them in the form of the commandments. The Children of Israel are about to renew their covenant with the LORD before entering into the Promised Land. In the midst of this, Moses tells them:

> The hidden [things] belong to the LORD our God, but the [things that are] revealed belong to us and to our children forever, that we may do all the words of this Torah. (Deuteronomy 29:28 [29])

Most commentators understand this passage to be speaking about various types of sins. The "hidden" are the types of sins in a person's life that are done unwittingly and have not been revealed yet. According to this interpretation, a person is not responsible for those sins. They are the LORD's responsibility, as the Psalmist states, "Who can discern his errors? Cleanse me from hidden faults" (Psalm 19:13). Obvious sins—"revealed" ones—however, we are personally responsible for.

However, I would like to suggest an alternate interpretation of the hidden and the revealed. What if they are the responsibilities of the two beings that support and sustain the world: the responsibility of God and the responsibility of man? Maybe we should think of the hidden things as the underworkings of Creation, the hidden components of physical existence. As we know, these are entirely in the hands of Hashem. We have no control over them. But the revealed things are something entirely different. These are the things that place the world's existence into our own hands. According to Simeon the Righteous, our responsibility to ensure against the collapse of the world has three components:

> He used to say, "On three things the world stands: on the Torah, on the (Temple) Service, and on acts of lovingkindness." (Avot 1:2)

Since we are living in a non-Temple period, we need to understand Temple Service as fixed times of daily prayer. Since the priests cannot currently perform their services in the Holy Temple, the responsibility has shifted to us. We must render the "bulls of our lips" (Hosea 14:2) in place of the lambs that were offered twice daily in the House of the LORD. Daily prayer is our service to the LORD.

Therefore, these three elements that support the world are (1) the study of Torah, (2) fixed times of daily prayer, and (3) acts of lovingkindness. These are the three components that undergird the existence of our world. Currently, each of these three spiritual components is deficient to its own degree. One day, however, this world will be perfected and returned to the ideal state. In that day the Torah, the Temple Service, and acts of lovingkindness will be returned to their proper proportions and Messiah Yeshua will reign over the earth from Jerusalem.

Until that time, we are responsible for making sure each of these three elements is sustained, rather than relying on others for their endurance. To work toward this ideal, every follower of Yeshua should be engaged in daily Torah study, fixed times of daily prayer, and acts of kindness as our minimum devotion to our Master. We can't do anything about the hidden, but we can definitely do something about the revealed. Will you help support the world today?

Parashat Vayelech

DEUTERONOMY 31:1-30

A Recipe For Rebellion

Parashat Vayelech, one of the shortest portions in the Torah, is only thirty verses long. However, if we look carefully, we can find within it a recipe for rebellion:

> For I know how rebellious and stubborn you are. Behold, even today while I am yet alive with you, you have been rebellious against the LORD. How much more after my death! (Deuteronomy 31:27)

This passage is written as a *kal vachomer*, an argument going from the light to the heavy: If A is true, then how much more so is B also true. Moses recognized that if the Children of Israel rebelled and strayed against the Torah's instruction while he was with them to take them by the hand and guide them in its requirements, how much more would they stray from it after his death? But who rebels against God's commands, and why?

There are generally two types of rebels. The first is the one who simply denies the truth and the authority of the Scripture and walks in outright rebellion against it. This is nothing spectacular. Rebels like this will exist in every generation that follows this path.

Parashat Vayelech

The second type, however, is one who claims that Scripture is still authoritative, yet rationalizes his behavior based on his own interpretations, rather than following the *mesorah*, the accepted interpretations and traditions. This is the more deceptive road to a wayward life. Let's explore the implications of this.

During the days of Moses, gaining understanding of a particular matter of Torah was easy for people. They could ask their questions and get an answer "straight from the horse's mouth." Moses, the very one who transmitted the teaching of Torah, was with them and could authoritatively answer their questions. In our modern world, however, we don't have the luxury of having Moses here to guide us and give us the "original" meaning of each and every passage of the Torah. So what do we do? Some may say, "We don't need Moses. We have the Ruach HaKodesh (the Holy Spirit) to lead us into all truth!" But if it is as simple as that, why do we have thousands of opposing interpretations and applications of the Scriptures from people claiming to be following the Holy Spirit, rather than a single, unified one? Is this truly the leading of the Spirit of God, or our own spirit of stubbornness? Paul says that we are to cling to the mesorah that he passed down:

> So then, brothers, stand firm and hold to the traditions that you were taught by us, either by our spoken word or by our letter. (2 Thessalonians 2:15)

Tradition and traditional interpretations are not inherently bad. They often keep us from falling off the path and into the ditch. They keep us from following after our own way when we want to follow the easier route. Judaism has an unending supply of mesorah designed to help maintain proper interpretation and application of Torah. But is bucking against tradition really an act of rebellion?

Stubbornness (or being "stiff-necked," as it literally reads) is a trait that signifies going one's own way. Rather than yielding to the designated authority, a stiff-necked person follows his own path, making his own rules and living by his own values. Proverbs says, "A fool takes no pleasure in understanding, but only in expressing his opinion" (Proverbs 18:2). A fool continues to say, "I don't think it means that," whereas wisdom listens to the counsel of many advisors (Proverbs 11:14).

Can there ever be new interpretations of Scripture? Yes. But they can never supersede the *pashat*—the plain sense of the text. For instance, the Torah says, "You shall kindle no fire in all your dwelling places on the Sabbath day" (Exodus 35:3). A midrashic interpretation based off of this verse says we should not engage in quarreling on the Sabbath. However, if we interpret this to apply *only* to quarreling and ignore the literal meaning of the text, then we have uprooted the foundation of the Torah. In Yeshua's words, we have "abolished" it.

Unfortunately, many people have chosen to take this approach. Why? Because it's comfortable and easy. We believe that if we obey the "spirit" of the law, then we can ignore the "letter" of the law. But this is not how it works. In order to obey the spirit of the law, one first has to obey the letter. Only when one first obeys the literal meaning of the commandment and then goes above and beyond its requirement does he fulfill the spirit of the law. To ignore either the pashat or the mesorah, one is simply walking in a more comfortable form of rebellion.

Moses is gone. We can choose to live out the Torah based on our own understandings, or turn to the wisdom of those who have gone before us and handed down both interpretation and tradition that have withstood the test of time. The choice is ours.

Parashat Ha'azinu

DEUTERONOMY 32:1-52

Two Witnesses

This week's Torah portion is only a single chapter long. The Ha'azinu, the Song of Moses, spans all fifty-two verses of our Torah portion. When reading this parashah, several questions come up. We will have time to answer only a few at this time.

First, in a Torah scroll, the Song of Moses is written in two columns rather than one. Why does this passage merit this unique rendering? The song opens with these words:

> Give ear, O heavens, and I will speak, and let the earth hear the words of my mouth. (Deuteronomy 32:1)

Moses introduces this song by calling upon two witnesses: the heavens and the earth. The Torah sets a precedent that a matter is established only by the testimony of two or more witnesses (Deuteronomy 19:15). By calling on both the heavens and the earth, Moses establishes his two witnesses against the Children of Israel to hold them accountable for their actions. The two columns of the Torah scroll are a reminder of this fact: two witnesses are being called to the stand; two witnesses are watching the Children of the Most High at all times.

Parashat Ha'azinu

Second, why does Moses ask both the heavens and the earth to listen to him? Why are the heavens and the earth called to be witnesses against humans? Just before giving us the details of the creation of man in Genesis 2, the Torah tells us that man is the combined product of both heaven and earth:

> These are the generations [*toldot*] of the heavens and the earth. (Genesis 2:4)

The word *toldot* can mean generations, offspring, genealogy, etc. Man was made as a combination of both heaven and earth when the Creator breathed a small portion of Himself into the dust of the earth. Heaven and earth, therefore, are partially responsible to oversee the actions of mankind.

Finally, why does Moses use two separate phrases referring to hearing? He says, "Give ear, O heavens" and, "Let the earth hear." What is the point of these two expressions? According to the Midrash, God has created the world in pairs:

> God said to Israel: "My children, all that I have created I have created in pairs; heaven and earth are a pair; sun and moon are a pair; Adam and Eve are a pair; this world and the world to come are a pair; but My Glory is One and unique in the world." How do we know this? From what we have read, Hear, O Israel: the LORD our God, the LORD is one. (Deuteronomy 6:4) (Deuteronomy Rabbah 2:31)

Just as the LORD created the various aspects of the world in pairs, when man was created he was given a pair of ears. We were given two ears and only one mouth, because we are supposed to be "quick to listen and slow to speak" (James 1:19). We were given two ears and only one heart so that we might hear the LORD's commandments and follow them with a single heart, as it is written, "Give me understanding, that I may keep your law and observe it with my whole heart" (Psalm 119:34).

When we proclaim, "Hear O Israel" as we recite the Shema, we testify to the LORD's sovereignty over our lives. When we pray the Amidah (the "standing" prayer) at mincha (afternoon prayers) and say, "When I proclaim the name of the LORD, ascribe greatness to our God!" (v. 3), we are strengthening our resolve to walk in His ways. Just as the heavens and earth are called to witness against us, these two sections of our prayers function as witnesses to our heart. As we speak them, the words travel from our mouth to our ears, our two witnesses.

Do you struggle to resist your flesh? Then pray. When we pray daily, we speak the words of Scripture from our mouth into our ears. If we are faithful and commit to this daily discipline, the Words of Life will eventually penetrate from our ears into our hearts. How do we know this to be true? Because "faith comes from hearing, and hearing through the word of God" (Romans 10:17). Therefore, may our lips confess the LORD's greatness to our ears, and our ears be witnesses that call us to a life of repentance and faith.

Parashat Vezot Ha'Bracha

DEUTERONOMY 33:1-34:12

The Loving Inheritance

In our morning prayers, one of the first passages of Scripture we recite is this: *Torah tzivah lanu Moshe morashah kehillat Yaakov—The Torah Moses commanded for us is a possession for the congregation of Jacob.* This is taken from our current Torah portion:

> Yes, he loved his people, all his holy ones were in his hand; so they followed in your steps, receiving direction from you, when Moses commanded us a law, as a possession for the assembly of Jacob. Thus the LORD became king in Jeshurun, when the heads of the people were gathered, all the tribes of Israel together. (Deuteronomy 33:3–5)

This passage should remind us of a few things. First, it reminds us that the Torah was an inheritance given to the Children of Israel through the hand of Moses. It was not given to them as a ball and chain, or a burden, or a mockery ("You can't keep it!"), but a loving inheritance from the One who delivered them from the yoke of slavery. The Torah is a gift from Hashem to a redeemed people in order to define the parameters of what it means to live a righteous life.

Second, this passage reminds us not only that we are to always

Parashat Vezot Ha'Bracha

give another person the benefit of the doubt even when they have let us down multiple times, but also that we can never become who we were intended to be until we are unified with our brothers and sisters. How do we derive this interpretation? Let's look at the very next verse:

> Thus the LORD became king in Jeshurun, when the heads of the people were gathered, all the tribes of Israel together. (Deuteronomy 33:5)

This verse is unique in that it calls Israel by an unusual name, Jeshurun. This word is used only four times in the entire Bible, and three of the four are found in these final words of Moses. Jeshurun (Hebrew *Yeshurun*) is a word that means "upright." Moses uses this term to describe the Children of Israel in their ideal state, a nation who is wholly upright and righteous before the LORD. Although Israel has had less than a perfect track record throughout its forty years between Sinai and where they stood at the border of the Promised Land, Hashem holds out hope for them by seeing only their potential future and not their stained past.

Commenting on the phrase, "when the heads of the people were gathered," Rashi cites an ancient commentary to show that Israel can become Jeshurun only when they are united:

> When Israel is gathered together in a unified group, and there is peace among them, God is their King, but not when there is strife among them. (Rashi, referencing Sifrei Devarim 346)

A little later in this passage in Sifrei, it adds, "when they constitute one unit, and not when they are divided into many factions." Although the Jewish people in the time of Yeshua were absorbed in performing the duties prescribed by the Torah, they were divided into many factions. Eventually, the Zealots brought down the hand of Rome upon Jerusalem and the entire population of Israel through their infighting and terrorist activities among even their Jewish brothers and sisters. Yeshua testifies to this by warning his disciples, "Beware of the scribes, who like to walk around in long robes, and love greetings in the marketplaces and the best seats in the synagogues and the places of honor at feasts, who devour widows' houses and for a pretense make long prayers" (Luke 20:46–47). This is why Jewish literature is able to claim that the Second Temple was destroyed due to *sinat chinam*, baseless hatred.

John says it this way:

> If anyone says, "I love God," and hates his brother, he is a liar; for he who does not love his brother whom he has seen cannot love God whom he has not seen. And this commandment we have from him: whoever loves God must also love his brother. (1 John 4:20–21)

When we are religiously devout and a staunch seeker of truth, but can't get along with our brothers and sisters, then we are nothing more than a spectacle and a stumbling block. Paul wanted his disciples at Corinth to understand this principle and gave them one of the most beautiful insights into this principle in his famous "Chapter of Love":

> If I speak in the tongues of men and of angels, but have not love, I am a noisy gong or a clanging cymbal. And if I

have prophetic powers, and understand all mysteries and all knowledge, and if I have all faith, so as to remove mountains, but have not love, I am nothing. If I give away all I have, and if I deliver up my body to be burned, but have not love, I gain nothing. (1 Corinthians 13:1–3)

When will Hashem be King over Jeshurun? When love and unity are the fruits of the people of God. Let's start today by building bridges rather than burning them, and loving our neighbor as ourselves.

Chazak! Chazak! V'nitchazeik! **Be strong! Be strong! And may we be strengthened!**